D1287018

Information Ethics for Librarians

Information Ethics for Librarians

MARK ALFINO
and
LINDA PIERCE

McFarland & Company, Inc., Publishers
Jefferson, North Carolina, and London

British Library Cataloguing-in-Publication data are available

Library of Congress Cataloguing-in-Publication Data

Alfino, Mark, 1959–
    Information ethics for librarians / Mark Alfino and Linda Pierce.
       p.   cm.
    Includes bibliographical references and index.
    ISBN 0-7864-0376-4 (library binding : 55# alk. paper) ∞
    1. Librarians—Professional ethics.   2. Information technology—
Moral and ethical aspects.   3. Information science—Moral and
ethical aspects.   4. Information scientists—Professional ethics.
5. Library science—Moral and ethical aspects.
I. Pierce, Linda, 1954–   . II. Title.
Z682.35.P75A44   1997
174'.9092—dc21   97-29606
                                                                CIP

Manufactured in the United States of America

McFarland & Company, Inc., Publishers
  Box 611, Jefferson, North Carolina 28640

Table of Contents

Preface

While some mystery is lost by a candid introduction of the authors, the compensation may be a clearer understanding of the work which follows. In part of our argument, we will claim that a clearer sense of what a librarian is and should be, and how a librarian should work through ethical challenges, can only be gained by understanding the historical and social context of the profession. While not a particularly novel claim, the method it implies should probably be applied self-referentially to the authors.

Linda Pierce, a librarian, and Mark Alfino, a philosopher, are on the faculty of Gonzaga University in Spokane, Washington. We have collaborated on a variety of projects, from pedagogically oriented work on the use of technology in the classroom to more philosophical discussion about the nature of information and librarianship. This latter interest developed into a team taught course on the philosophy of information. While that course had a general focus, at some point it became clear to us that a philosophical understanding of the nature of information could be part of the foundation for a comprehensive rethinking of the information ethics of librarianship. This book is the product of that rethinking.

Three specific sources of motivation bear mention here. The first was a dissatisfaction with a typical approach to ethics which, useful in its own way, is rather limited. That approach might be called "hot issue" ethics or "serialized ethics" because it treats ethical issues as a series of discrete dilemmas that intrude on an otherwise ethically neutral or settled practice. A patron asks for information that we feel, personally, is inappropriate for them, yet we are professionally obligated to help them find it. In the course of a normal sales visit, a vendor of periodical databases indicates that we might receive a "premium" for purchasing a specific product. No doubt, ethical problems often feel just this discrete and intrusive to everyday life: we remember the moment before we found ourselves in a quandary, and we know what brought on the problem. We convey this sense to others by the way we relate ethical experiences as specific stories about our actual or hypothetical experience.

As important as it is to confront ethical problems head on, we both felt

1

that something was missing in the discussion of professional ethics even after one had treated and disposed of a long series of what-would-you-do-if scenarios. Most people handle hot ethical issues by drawing on deeper values. When we disagree about the discrete issues, it often happens that we differ in our interpretation of the more basic values. It is also possible that we can agree with someone on a course of action and only later find out that the bases of that agreement were different and incompatible views of the more fundamental values. Since time is a scarce commodity, we usually do not delve into the subterrain of our professional moral commitments. When we started to notice, however, that much published work in library ethics had an insufficiently critical awareness of its own basic value commitments, we decided it might be time well spent to explore the "foundations" of information ethics with librarianship in mind. A motivation of our work in this book, then, is a feeling that, to borrow a phrase, "the way up is the way down"; we will make progress in knowing where information ethics is headed by knowing its basis.

A second motivation for the present book is a change, still underway, in the way applied ethics is done. As we shall see in Chapter 1, a traditional approach in applied ethics is to directly apply traditional moral theories to specific moral problems. Though few doubt the relevance of such a common sense approach, the actual practice often lacks subtlety and does not always take into account the personal, social, and historical context of the ethical situation. In striving for universal solutions, philosophers often marginalize features of a moral problem which are nonetheless important. Under a variety of headings, including "narrative ethics," applied ethicists are at work to develop accounts of professional ethics which are sensitive to context. This work is both an example and test case of these new methods.

Finally, we would be hard pressed to deny that the enormous and fascinating changes in social life, information technology, and the structure of knowledge were not driving us toward a rethinking of how these very phenomena are affecting our understanding of librarianship and its professional practice. Hardly a day goes by without hearing about a new configuration of information technology that changes some practice or decision process which had formerly been settled. Librarians who once thought that information technology might merely pose new, potentially dramatic, means for accomplishing traditional library tasks must surely now acknowledge that technology has altered much more. Certainly, the means of organizing and accessing information have changed, but so have substantive issues about what information counts as knowledge, how one collects, and how the mission of the library and the profession integrates with other institutions. Not all of these changes are driven by information technology alone. Social attitudes toward libraries are in a state of flux as well. It is our contention that understanding the professional obligations of librarians will require new habits of thinking about these larger questions of social change.

At the outset, then, it should be easy to see how a work such as this risks exceeding its subject matter in an unmanageable way. To avoid this, the Introduction discusses several specific issues as a way of introducing the reader to our method of analysis and setting the stage for the more extended arguments of chapters 1 through 4.

Chapter 1 concerns itself with traditional moral theory and the relationship between that theory and ethical practice in librarianship. After this foundational work in information ethics, we turn in Chapter 2 to a study of the professional identity and organizational environment of librarianship. Our goal is to describe a new mission-centered view of the profession and recommend organizational structures appropriate to that view of professional identity.

In Chapter 3, we focus on another major source for reflection on librarianship: the social, political, and intellectual history of the profession, especially its development during the past hundred and fifty years in the United States. Though librarianship has a history of several millennia, we feel confident that it is the development of modern library practice in the contemporary United States political and social culture that provides the most important and immediately relevant lessons for understanding what a library is, and, hence, what a librarian is obligated to do. Some recent writers on the social history of the public library movement have keen insights on the formation of the librarian's professional ethos. Yet writers on the professional ethics of librarians rarely connect these two parts of library literature. It is our hope to exploit this connection in order to argue for a specific understanding of the various "professional callings" of different kinds of librarians.

The first two major pieces of the "information-ethics-for-librarians" puzzle are the philosophical ethics of information and the professional ethics of librarians. A third is organizational ethics. Almost all professional librarians work in organizations, and the character of the organization cannot be ignored in understanding the nature and duties of the profession. One of the incontrovertible successes of the professional and organizational ethics movement is to make good theoretical use of our intuition that the ethical culture of an organization is not just a sum of the ethical conduct of each individual in it. There is, alongside the individual's character, the *ethos* of the group, embodied in the official practices, divisions of labor, and policies of the organization. Good people can work for bad organizations. Organizational theory in ethics is focused, in part, on how to raise the likelihood that the organizations we work in will foster and allow the expression of the best ethical deliberation of its workers. What are the optimal forms of organization for librarian's work? A complete answer to this question must be informed by a study of the historical mission of the library. In Chapter 2, we will, however, give a preliminary analysis based on current thinking in organizational theory.

The final practical outcome of our study (in chapters 4 and 5) is to describe and defend an ideal of the librarian in the context of their professional practice in (primarily) library organizations. If we are successful, then our approach to resolving ethical problems will be responsive to the major moral challenges which librarians face today. The evidence of this success will be that some contemporary challenges and moral crises which occupy librarians today will be clarified, and the outlines of their solutions made visible. While our rationale for this project is based on a desire to think deeply about the most fundamental issues behind professional ethics for librarians—the moral importance of information, and the nature of organizational life, the nature of librarianship—we also want to show the practicality of the more abstract study by trying to resolve some practical moral problems. Chapter 4 will include both general practical discussions about how to institutionalize ethical reflection in library organizations and specific analyses of ethical issues such as neutrality, collections, and service. In a brief concluding chapter we will describe our integrated vision of the mission of the information age librarian.

In the process of researching this book, we made extensive use of the interlibrary loan services of the Foley Center at Gonzaga University. Connie Soms deserves special thanks for her help in tracking down sources. The entire Public Services Department at the Foley Center provided support and encouragement throughout the project. Gonzaga University supported our research through a grant from the Faculty Research Council and by awarding sabbatical leave to Linda. Finally, we would like to thank our spouses, Carl Hein and Michele Pajer, for their encouragement, patience, and support throughout this project.

Introduction

Rethinking Information Ethics for Librarians

Few doubt that we are living through a time of rapid technological and social change and that this change will affect not only the means by which we do our jobs, but also the definition and scope of our professions as well. In the day-to-day experience of this change, we tend to focus on very specific and apparently trivial things—whether new networking and computing systems work, how to send email, fax, and printing from one machine to another, how to share information and work cooperatively in an electronic environment. At close range, it is easy to feel that technological change is more about how we do our work than what our work is. As we shall argue at length in the coming chapters, this feeling is an illusion. If we pause to look at the long term, to reflect on the nature of professional librarianship in the context of its technical and social history, we will find that the daily increments of technical change, exhilarating and frustrating in their own right, are but the outward signs of a much more basic change in the nature, not just means, of librarianship.

The same could be said of many other social changes. In the short term, we focus on how new court cases affect our professional liability, how new alignments in local or state politics affect funding, how new requests or demands from patrons and other stakeholders alter our behavior and planning. Necessarily, we look at each of these developments in relation to our immediate practices and objectives. It may even occur to us at some point that the professional world we work in is, or has become, very different from the one for which we were originally educated. But the flow of our work requires short term adjustments to incremental changes and rarely gives us the opportunity to speculate about the overall effect of change on our professional mission. The overall effect of these changes is often much more profound than their sum.

Perhaps the most exciting thing about living through a time of great technological change is that the sources of anxiety and confusion are balanced, for the most part, by a feeling of great opportunity. One day we find out that a familiar and low cost library resource is discontinued or will take a new form in a more costly technology. The next day we read about a way of sharing information with more patrons and increasing opportunities for the use of libraries. With the possibility of pleasant surprise at the wealth of new information in online and Internet resources comes the discomfort, shock, or outrage at the prospect of supporting access, through the Internet, to low-quality and nonauthoritative sources of information.

It would be a mistake to think that external sources of change, technological or social, are always at the heart of the ethical dilemmas and confusions librarians face today. Professions have their own dynamic for change. Professionals who gather at conferences year after year and develop new programs and initiatives for patron service and technical skill will inevitably uncover new challenges and questions. In the intellectual freedom movement of the early 1960s, librarians had to sort through the moral concerns of patrons who felt that children should not have unrestricted access to the "adult" collection. If librarians felt moral confusion, torn perhaps between values of open intellectual inquiry and paternalism, it was not a confusion caused so much by a new technology or changing social forces as by the very practices of librarianship.

Ultimately, technological change is a kind of social change, though rooted in the development of new technique. Also, what are "professional practices" in librarianship but techniques of interacting, ultimately, with the society at large? Perhaps there is "pure" technical and "pure" professional change, but the kinds of change that lead to moral confusion, that lead to worries about professional ethics are all changes which have implications for social values. By sorting through the varieties of social change, we can begin to understand the forces that motivate "new" moral problems in professional ethics. The central argument for our approach to thinking about information ethics for librarians depends for its plausibility on an analysis of the sources of role confusion in library practice today.

What are some of the major ethical quandaries facing librarians today, and what are their sources? Perhaps the single most frequently cited "case" of information ethics for librarians is a "reference ethics" case created by librarian Robert Hauptman, while studying library science in 1975. He visited six public libraries and seven academic libraries seeking reference help in locating information that would help him learn how to build a bomb. He was astounded to find that reference librarians in all 13 libraries readily acceded to his request (though one refused him service on grounds that he wasn't a student at the school served by the library). For good reason, the "Hauptman case" has become a textbook case of the conflict between personal and professional roles in librarianship. Should the librarian refuse the patron's request on ethical grounds? Should the librarian find out more about the patron's possible criminal intent? Is reference service a value-neutral professional activity which proscribes any considerations apart from the technical questions of how to access the information?[1]*

Our purpose at present is not to decide the case, but to consider its motivations. Is it technological change, social change, or changes in professional library practice that motivate the ethical conundrum? Reference service is a specific library practice which emerged in the 1890s[2] as an innovation in librarianship. In a sense, librarians made the dilemma possible by offering to mediate the patron's request in the first place. Of course, an ethical concern can still be raised when independent library users access inappropriate information. Ethical concerns about reference are ultimately heightened by three underlying social forces: the advanced organization of the fields of knowledge, the growth of publications which make knowledge of subjects such as bomb building "collectible," and the intellectual freedom movement, which preceded the Hauptman case by two decades.

After all, in a "simpler" time a librarian might honestly have replied that there were no volumes on the subject in the collection. While some early twentieth century public libraries focused on trades and practical arts, it would have been easier to avoid collecting bomb building information in a time when knowledge of that art was less well studied and discussed in print. There are more scientific and practical uses of explosives in applied engineering today than years ago. There are also more mainstream, yet politically radical, political journals and books today. Finally, given the contemporary understanding of free speech and the public's diminished willingness to tolerate prior restraint censorship, the "role confusion" of the reference librarian seems well accounted for.

One value to exploring the "motivations" of an ethical problem before attempting its solution is that we can ward off certain kinds of hasty inferences and sophisms at the outset. It is tempting to read the emergence of new ethical problems as a symptom of the "decline" of values. Sometimes this is justified, but in the Hauptman case, the cause may be a reprioritizing of values (intellectual freedom over personal ethics) and the general advance of organized retrievable knowledge. It is also tempting to think that new professional ethics problems reveal some loss of consensus within a profession about core professional values. However, in the Hauptman case it seems implausible to say that librarians somehow knew their professional values better in the early 20th century when in fact their practices and the social environment they worked in never permitted the problem to arise. In identifying the Hauptman case as an instance of contemporary "role confusion," we should not be taken

See Chapter Notes beginning on page 157.

as implying, therefore, that librarians somehow knew their way and then became morally lost.

Librarians are also concerned about recent changes in technology which have made it harder for them to discharge their responsibility for careful collections development. When knowledge was mostly collectible in bound volumes of relatively high cost, the decision to avoid collecting for marginal or less mainstream tastes and interests was easier. With the growth of serials, even before automated databases and the Internet, the ability to manage, qualitatively, the content of a library collection diminished. Current confusions over the extent to which the Internet's resources should available to patrons are but an expansion, of great proportion, of this original problem. Should librarians continue to exercise their traditional judgment over the quality of publication sources (and reject large packaged reference databases or open-ended sources like the World Wide Web) or honor their other professional value for maximizing the breadth and depth of information to patrons?

Again, in the confusion over collections policy in a technological age we might be tempted to say that librarians have lost an ability to collect appropriate materials, and that this is an ability that they used to have. But when we take a historical look at the way the moral confusion arises we are led to a different hypothesis. It may be that instead of no longer knowing how to do something we used to do well, we are now in the position of doing something very different (in collections), and yet we haven't realized what this new professional activity is or what professional values should guide it. In other words, the problem may not be that the "players" in the professional game have forgotten the "rules," as much as the nature of the game is changing. It is this view of contemporary role confusion in librarianship that motivates our call, in this book, for a rethinking of the basis of information ethics.

In looking at moral controversies in collection policy, the temptation is even greater to say that librarians used to have more consensus about the values guiding collection development. Indeed, there may be some truth to this, in spite of such long-standing controversies as the value of collecting popular fiction. But we shouldn't mistake agreement for moral legitimacy. If a 1920s library had greater agreement not to collect materials on communism or political radicalism, we might say they had greater consensus about their values, but, in retrospect, a narrower vision of their mission. By looking at the motivations of contemporary moral problems in professional librarianship we avoid some common assumptions about the "newness" of the root causes of the problems.

On the other hand, librarians do experience some kinds of moral confusion that were not latent in their predecessors' practices. Consider the way in which librarians serve on boards of networks, councils, and other governing bodies.[3] One might assume that service in mainstream professional organizations, such as the American Library Association, is always consistent with the interests of a professional's local employer, but librarians also serve in orga-nizations that set prices and policies for networking and cataloging services that may adversely affect the interests of their immediate employer. Such conflicts of interest are a common topic of professional ethics, yet conflict of interest scenarios for librarians have received limited discussion in library lit-erature.[4]

The examples mentioned above were chosen from a long list of ethics topics in professional life today. Looking at the full range of ethics issues that concern librarians, we see many cases which reveal weaknesses in long held assumptions about professional values. We have already mentioned the prob-lem of control of collections. This challenges a long-standing assumption that local librarians can and should deploy their skills to cultivate and catalog mate-rials appropriate to their communities and constituents. While there has been no wholesale abandonment of this value, the structure of new information technologies and the emergence of shared cataloging call the traditional under-standing of this value into question.

Questioning Assumptions: Value Neutrality and Bias in Scholarly Communication

Librarians raised in the era of intellectual freedom are also questioning assumptions about the "value neutrality" of reference service work. The stan-dard word on the subject of the value neutrality doctrine is D. J. Foskett's 1962 book, *The Creed of a Librarian—No Politics, No Religion, No Morals*. He writes, for example, that "During the reference service, the librarian ought virtually to vanish as an individual person, except in so far as his personality sheds light on the working of the library."[5] A less dramatic, yet more official expression of value neutrality can be found in the current American Library Association Code of Ethics, which begins with a call for "accurate, unbiased, and courte-ous responses to all requests."[6]

What value could be more sacred, and in less need of revisiting, in pro-fessional librarianship, than the "value neutrality" value? After all, was value neutrality not one of the principle achievements of the intellectual freedom movement of the early 1960s? Not withstanding any qualms one might feel about the Hauptman or Dowd cases, would anyone prefer to have reference librarians substitute their judgment for the patron's about the appropriateness of a patron's request?

Sophisticated challenges to the value neutrality assumption are often quite theoretical, but by following them we can gain practical insights into the state of librarian ethics. As Gillian Gremmels discusses in "Reference in the Public Interest: An Examination of Ethics,"[7] we have to consider arguments that suggest that value neutrality is not possible and does not serve the public interest. The problem is not just that it is hard to be neutral, but rather that it is an impossible, fundamentally self-deceptive goal. Before considering what the practical alternatives to this position are, let us consider Gremmels' arguments in some depth.

Underlying the belief that neutrality is a theoretically possible ideal is the assumption that the contours of reality are relatively fixed independent of human involvement, rather than essentially interpreted or constructed within a social and historical set of human concerns. Only with a fixed reference point of unvarnished facts could one determine what neutrality means. Neutrality may be a practical ideal within the context of scientific method (though many philosophers of science argue persuasively that our scientific paradigms are riddled with culturally contingent ideologies), but in fields of general knowledge and cultural works that most nontechnical library activity occurs, it is hard to maintain that knowledge is not structured by specific interpretive interests. On this view, any reference librarian who feels that they are merely facilitating a direct relationship between the patron and "knowledge of reality as it is" is self-deceived. At best, reference librarians are, in the name of neutrality, perpetuating the biases of the research communities and prevailing cultural ideologies dominant in the library's collection.

The deeper intellectual sources for Gremmels' argument are contemporary theorists in the social sciences, especially in ethnomethodology, where many researchers feel more productive results come from acknowledging bias as an intrinsic feature of the research project. The results one obtains from abandoning the assumption of objectivity in social reality are less generalizable, but since interpretive social scientists argue that such objectivity is illusory, they naturally do not feel that much is lost in the trade off.

On a practical level, Gremmels argues, the illusion of value neutrality leads librarians to deny their involvement in a political and social world, and to deny the implications of that involvement. Consider the follow vignette which illustrates, for the author, the untenability of value neutrality as a professional ideal:

> A citizen group in a middle-class neighborhood had been formed ... because a massage parlor was opening in a small commercial strip which included a branch library, an insurance firm, and a group of shops. Neighborhood church, school and business leaders rallied with neighborhood citizens in support of the new group's opposition to the opening of the massage parlor. Yet, when the library was asked for help, the response both of the branch librarian and the central administration to the request was that the library could not assist the group due to the library's neutral role in the community.[8]

In this case, the library administration self-consciously removed itself from a local political process in the name of neutrality. However, it is hard to imagine that their abstinence had a neutral effect. The core of the practical argument against value neutrality can be seen clearly in this example: value neutrality is itself a value with often predictable and non-neutral implications for the outcomes of the library profession's involvement in public life and the life of its patrons. As one value among many, its value must be weighed against the values of competing interests.

Perhaps this should be viewed as an extreme example in which value neutrality as an ideal in reference service has been misplaced into the context of the public administration of the library which, no one could deny, involves arguing forcefully in the political process for the ideals of the library. But is it easy to make a sharp distinction between the arenas in which librarians should articulate their professional values and those in which they should not? In what professional context should librarians deny that they believe "information is a useful commodity, a good thing ... [and] that it is better to be literate than illiterate"?[9] These may seem like innocuous and inoffensive values, but it is not hard to see how their deployment could collide with a mainstream version of value-neutral reference service. When an actual patron (not a librarian conducting an ethics experiment) comes to ask for information on free-basing cocaine, does value neutrality require the librarian to refrain from also suggesting sources on the health risks of cocaine use? When a patron seeks information to build a case for abortion rights, is it inappropriate for librarians, who believe it is better to be informed than uninformed, to suggest sources which present alternative perspectives?

One hears an echo of Gremmels' argument in discussions of bias in information technology. Commenting on Foskett's statement of neutrality, Thomas Froehlich writes:

> It is often asserted that information specialists should be neutral with respect to the information they provide.... This seems fair enough: the specialist should subscribe to no party's viewpoint and should avoid bias in difficult matters, by providing a wide range of materials on such matters. But such a view of neutrality is naive, because the provision only occurs from that which is only and already available in the system and within the context of the information technologies and technological practices that constitute the system, including the specialist.[10]

Many writers on technology, including Froehlich, Jacques Ellul, and others, as well as philosophers such as Martin Heidegger and Jürgen Habermas, have argued forcefully that technology is not value neutral and that it hardly presents an unobtrusive means of mediating our relationship to the world. With the pervasiveness of information technology in librarianship, and with the development of its complexity in organizing knowledge, we have every reason to doubt that librarians will be able to maintain the view that "value neutrality" at the point of service to the patron somehow guarantees the patron a direct relationship to knowledge of reality.

Our goal is not, at this stage in our argument, to decide in favor or against the complex arguments which have been only briefly sketched here. We will return to the value neutrality issue later in the book (see page 117). Our thesis has been that credible arguments have been advanced to call the professional assumption of value neutrality into question. Since this assumption motivates a wide range of discrete ethical dilemmas discussed in the professional literature, it is important for us to isolate it here to illustrate a distinctive feature of our method in discussing the information ethics of librarianship. Instead of starting with the ethical incident, as the Hauptman and Dowd experiments have encouraged writers on this subject to do, we want to begin by identifying, on a more theoretical level, some of the issues which form the basis for any answer to professional ethics quandaries.

This approach is more difficult, and it requires holding in abeyance the natural desire to "settle" concrete issues, but it promises a deeper and more comprehensive rethinking of professional values. To see more of the implications of our approach, consider the following response to the information scientists' argument that information technology and delivery systems have inherent biases. A reasonable and practical librarian might reply that bias in the structure of knowledge and information technology is unfortunate, but not relevant to the librarian's main task in reference service: to facilitate the patrons' use of the library's resources. No doubt it is an illusion to believe that those resources are without bias, but, the argument goes, so also is it an illusion to think that librarians can do much about that, beyond collecting resources which represent many competing views. Such a response sidesteps both the theoretical and practical arguments against neutrality discussed above by focusing our attention on the immediate context of the service delivery. In that context, one has to use the word "neutrality" in a limited sense, to mean "neutral with respect to the available resources." With this proviso, one can avoid the charge of self-deception and naïveté.

What makes this response seem reasonable is that it takes a realistic and practical understanding of the constraints of most librarians' work as the basis for limiting the analysis of the ethical problem. One can imagine a UPS driver having the same lack of interest in discussing traffic engineering: his or her job is the delivery of a specific service within the constraints posed by other service providers. However, it is not intellectually credible to begin the argument by assuming a fixed conception of the line between the librarian's professional concerns and others. Many of the best "solutions" to professional ethics problems involve altering the mix of duties and obligations of the professional.[11] Even if many librarians will never be in a position to affect the structure of knowledge in information technology, why shouldn't librarianship as a profession be actively involved with such questions?[12] What view of the nature of librarianship is assumed in the "practical" reply?

At the heart of our approach to information ethics for librarians is the claim, suggested in the line of argument just discussed, that satisfactory treatments of serious information ethics issues raise questions of professional identity. Only in light of an analysis of what an information provider is and what kinds of information providers librarians are can one give credible answers to the ethical problems librarians face in handling information. To understand what an information provider is we need some understanding of the value of information to individuals. To understand what kind of information provider a librarian is we need to understand the organizations within which most librarians work and scan the history of librarianship for telling and insightful moments where the profession seems to have wrestled with its core identity.

Several other important assumptions of librarianship are in question today, such as the assumption that the publicly supported library is in a unique position to satisfy the information needs of a community. As private information services proliferate, more information providers see the library as one of their main competitors. As libraries try to supply the technical information needs of the business community, often offering fee-based services to specific clients, they ironically blur the line between the public function of the library and the market-based concept of commodified information. Thus, pressure arises from sources both internal and external to the profession for a clearer understanding of the need for publicly subsidized libraries. At one level this is a public policy debate, tangled up with contemporary questions about the role of government. At another level, justification of the public mandate of the library has been a long-standing object of reflection within the profession: Whose needs do we serve? Whose information needs should be satisfied in the private market? Ironically, as the information expertise of professional librarians evolves, they become increasingly able to, and often more interested in, developing new markets for their services, especially among constituencies ready and willing to pay the publicly subsidized fees for that information.

Another assumption under fire concerns the relationship between the librarian and the publishing industry. Traditionally, the library community is a client of the "knowledge and culture industry," at least of that sizeable part of its production that is routinely collected by libraries. When publishers argue that "cooperative acquisitions" programs violate fair use, they are relying on a traditional conception of this client and provider relationship. Some of the great changes occurring in the production and distribution of published information are leading us to ask not only "What is a client?" but "What is a publication?" When should self-publication, now so easy and effective in distributing documents, retain its traditional stigma as a form of "vanity publishing"? When the editors of an authoritative traditional publication have been found negligent in the execution of their own standards for peer review or when they have violated norms of academic freedom, should librarians take any action?[13] Given the library's involvement in validating and perpetuating the reputation of a publication by continued collection, one might argue that librarians have a professional obligation to take some action.

In order to satisfy their professional obligation to make some effort toward assuring the accuracy of the information they collect, librarians have traditionally used review sources and their own judgment to assess the integrity of a publication. New and complex ownership patterns of traditional publishing houses make it harder to infer the character or quality of a work from its publication source. Old standards for evaluating the integrity of a publication are harder to apply in a corporate and technological environment in which the reputations of editors are becoming harder to establish.

Even apart from these larger changes, how should librarians decide that they have satisfied their obligation to collect and disseminate accurate information? Since peer review prior to publication is typically confidential, librarians have little means of knowing whether such reviews were carried out with integrity or whether they were carried out at all. If journal editors lead readers to believe that their publications are blind reviewed, or that they have a certain selectivity (many journals publish, with pride, their rejection rates), and librarians later find that articles have been rejected without consideration (based on a disregard for the author), what, if anything, should they do? The traditional approach is to let peer reviewers in the specific fields of knowledge sort out their own scandals, and to wait for rectification of misconduct. This, for example, is the position advanced by C. Osborn in "The Structuring of Scholarly Communication."[14] But as Gordon Moran and Michael Mallory argue in "Some Ethical Considerations Regarding Scholarly Communication," such an approach "does not sufficiently acknowledge that the history of science and other fields, to a large degree, constitutes a history of academic whistle-blowing…. Thus, scientific progress and changing theories are natural enemies of authoritarian tradition."[15] Most librarians consistently endorse the principle that a full range of opinions on academic controversies should be represented in a collection—but does that principle only refer to the range of opinions by competing academic authorities, each with their own established sources of dissemination, or does it extend further to include renegades, intellectual malcontents, and so-called academic whistle blowers?

To give this issue one last philosophical twist, we should point out that discussions of the librarian's possible complicity in biased scholarship occur against the backdrop of significant changes in the way we explain the evolution and transformation of different paradigms of knowledge. Since the publication of Thomas Kuhn's *The Structure of Scientific Revolutions*, faith in the traditional picture of "normal science" has been undermined. Many historians of science now accept Kuhn's sociological reading of the history of science, according to which scientific paradigms are displaced in radical upheavals and shifts in fundamental ways of thinking. Using Moran's and Mallory's terminology, Kuhnians might say that "academic whistle blowing" is the norm for scientific paradigm shifts. Thus, quiescence on the part of librarians may positively impair the emergence of new paradigms of knowledge. Does the loss of the traditional assumption of the slow and steady progress of knowledge in favor or Kuhn's revolutionary model have implications for the roles of librarians in the academic disputes of the various disciplines?

Again, as with the value neutrality discussion, well-meaning librarians could argue that it simply is not their business to champion or publicize the causes of fringe thinkers and researchers in the various disciplines. Even if the standard review sources in a discipline are dominated by an entrenched group, the librarian's job is to make the best judgment about what to collect on the basis of existing review sources. As in our earlier case, we can acknowledge the reasonableness and practicality of this response while objecting that it assumes an understanding of the professional identity of the librarian that may not be valid. Why assume that librarians are professionally incompetent to enter the fray of discipline-specific disputes?

Over and again, in our review of librarians' professional ethics, we encountered an approach which seemed to imply that librarians were passive captives of larger forces—the demands of patrons, the changing values of the community, the needs and authority of "knowledge workers" in the various disciplines—that limited their sphere of activity. It is as though the unacknowledged method for settling ethical issues in librarianship were to begin by determining what it is "practical" for a librarian to do by consulting primarily the parties the librarian serves. While it would be wrong to ignore the requests of those constituents, especially to the extent that librarianship is a service profession, it would also be wrong to "sell short" the independent and authoritative judgment of the librarian about the structure and organization of knowledge.

Librarians in Relationship to Knowledge and Technology

Having considered some of the moral role confusions and questioned assumptions in librarianship today, we are in a better position to describe two of the fundamental relationships underlying both questions of professional identity and the motivation of contemporary information ethics problems for librarians. By tracing out these relationships, we can move information ethics from a practical exercise in managing constraints to a more philosophical deliberation over the nature of librarianship in the broader relationship of human beings to information. Our minimal assumption is that librarianship is a profession which mediates the human experience of information.[16] To add content to this initial intuition, we will look on the one hand to our broad study of information in Chapter 1 and on the other hand to our historical and sociological analysis of the library profession in Chapter 3. A related question, "How is the work of this mediation organized?" will be addressed in Chapter 2.

One "deep assumption" in both the popular imagination and in professional literature is that the librarian's relationship to knowledge is relatively passive, like the stamp collector's relationship to stamp production, or the audience's relationship to the performers on a stage. In the theater of knowledge productions, librarians are avid spectators, but always spectators. When we look at the history of the profession, we will see some explanations for this, but from a conceptual standpoint, it is easy to see how this picture emerged. After all, "library science" does not seem, to most people, to produce a knowledge of its own, except the technical knowledge of cataloging or the study of the use of libraries themselves. The discipline's relationship to knowledge cannot, therefore, be parallel to other disciplines.

This way of thinking about the librarian's relationship to knowledge is more suited to an earlier epoch of librarianship than to that of today. If we could credibly think about knowledge as produced in many independent disciplines and then "reported" to the library via the publishing industry, then it might make sense to reinforce the older stereotype of the librarian as the warehouse worker of the knowledge industry. But several developments in the structure of knowledge, including the growth of interdisciplinary studies, collaboration in research, and theoretical accounts of the "sociology of knowledge" lead us to think of the library's resources more as a medium of knowledge production than merely a record of it.

The fertility of interdisciplinary studies, enriched by not only new findings that result from borrowing among the disciplines but also (in what might be called "intradisciplinary" studies) from transferring knowledge across formerly isolated subfields within a discipline, depends upon scholars gaining access to, and understanding, the technical or specialized results of many different fields of knowledge. Many interdisciplinary scholars are by temperament the sort of people who can see connections among disparate fields and their incongruous vocabularies. Librarianship plays an active role in organizing knowledge for interdisciplinary use. As the objectives of researchers in the disciplines of knowledge change, the role of the librarian in knowledge production become more prominent.

One might think that this phenomenon is limited to the humanities and, perhaps, the social sciences. However, the way in which scientists collaborate in research also highlights a new and active role for librarians in the production of knowledge. The primary source data used in scientific study are increasingly a part of the library's collection. Student patrons can access scientific databases and in some cases follow the progress of scientific work as it is occurring. Where formerly researchers would circulate and compare research data within a more private research community, it now makes good research sense to have the process of producing the finished research work part of the collectible record.

The sheer growth of scientific research communities makes access to the base of research knowledge less a private and manageable task of the primary researcher and more the function of specialized members of research teams. As that happens, the "library" (in the broadest sense: the sources of public access to information and knowledge) will undertake more involvement in the process of knowledge production. This does not mean that librarians will become scientists (though there is a constant demand for librarians with discipline-specific knowledge), but it does mean that the expertise of the librarian in the organization of data and knowledge will play a crucial role in the production process for knowledge.

Finally, theoretical accounts of the structure and growth of knowledge, from Thomas Kuhn's *Structure of Scientific Revolutions* to François Lyotard's *The Postmodern Condition: A Report on Knowledge*, have emphasized the sociological context within which knowledge is produced. The more we study the development of different fields of knowledge (including, as we shall see, the field of librarianship), the more we become disabused of the traditional and naive prejudice that what drives the growth of knowledge is the simple encounter of a researcher with reality. Adequate explanations of the development of a way of knowing the world must make reference to the ways in which researchers reflect cultural assumptions, imperatives, and prejudices. This means that the history of the organization of a discipline is also an object of study and appraisal in rethinking the major paradigms of knowledge within the discipline. Since librarians reflect on the organization and structure of disciplines of knowledge, they are both excellent sources of information and good candidates to research these kinds of questions.

In general then, the librarian's relationship to knowledge may be shifting from a relatively passive, external relationship, like a critic or collector, to a more critical and involved participation in the process of research and the appraisal of knowledge communities. As the lines between "knowledge producer" and "knowledge collector" blur somewhat, we may find librarians better positioned to play substantive roles in the production and validation of knowledge.

Some of this prognostication applies more directly to the academic librarian, to be sure. For many public librarians, the line between passivity and activity was crossed decades ago, though with respect to a slightly different distinction. Modern and well-funded public libraries are sources of tremendous activity in the application, though not so much the production, of knowledge. Creative library programs inevitably involve content expertise and move librarians from the role of consumers (and proxy consumers) to professional producers, like professors and researchers, who manipulate data, information, and knowledge to create novel presentations and effects in their audiences. Ultimately, this activity is a form of local culture, more or less parasitic on other producers depending upon the creativity, talent, and resources of the librarian and his or her organization.

In sketching the librarian's relationship to technology, we are partly interested in describing the role that technology plays in motivating ethical issues and partly interested in understanding how the introduction of technology will or should alter the librarian's professional identity. Under the first heading, we have already seen how tempting it is to identify technology as the "culprit" in a host of technology-related ethics issues. One illusion of this approach is that it leads us to suppose that librarians once had greater moral clarity about their profession, when the truth may rather be that their moral responses were never tested because the contemporary problem is, indeed, novel. So at the outset we could say that when technology creates novel ethical problems, it performs a diagnostic function in the moral life of the professional. New information technology puts pressure on our general values and forces us to think through new applications of them. In the process, we find out what it really means, in practice, to believe in core values such as the value of literacy, critical inquiry, intellectual freedom, or the social mission of the library.

Information technology does not merely present new ethical dilemmas of the "what-would-you-do-if..." variety; it also requires us to reprioritize our values. Because information technology changes the cost structure of some kinds of collections, and because it involves a commitment to resources which favor some patrons' needs over others, it will always force us to reconsider the relative importance of serving various constituents. Should more patrons be required to learn basic computer skills to access information online? Should the added costs of network technology to make off site OPAC access available be taken from resources that "low tech" walk-in patrons use? Certainly, there are many win-win outcomes from new technology, but in an environment of scarce resources, information technology which does not lower overall costs will necessarily force a reconsideration of our service mission as librarians.

The larger stakes in the librarian's relationship to technology have to do with the effect of technology on professional identity. The forms of information technology that have had the greatest and most widespread impact on libraries are automated cataloging systems, public access catalogs, electronic serials indexes and document delivery systems, and automated search engines and indexes such as those found on the Internet. While none of these technologies are full-fledged "expert systems," cybernetic approximations of natural language reasoning and decision making processes, they may negatively alter professional relationships by removing a degree of independent judgment from the professional's activity.[17]

The promises and perils of automated cataloging are well discussed in the library literature. Using systems like OCLC or relying on CIP data for cataloging may reduce cataloging costs, though this results in the sacrifice of local idio-syncrasies in the library catalogue; these variations from a standard might have real value to local communities. The increased reliance on predefined or amal-gamated citation indexes may turn the librarian into a technician of the elec-tronic information system, reducing both the public's perception of the role of qualitative judgment in reference work and the professional status of the librarian.

One future for this scenario is to accept a technological vision of the librarian's work, and train librarians more like the way we train computer pro-grammers. While librarians' work is too diverse to generalize into a single image, one might imagine that most information-oriented reference work could be covered by this more technical view of librarianship. This informa-tion-technician librarian would be a professional expert in the use of auto-mated information technology, but would require less training and expertise in thinking about "philosophical issues" about service. We could then further segregate the expertise of library administrators to select information services from the expertise of public service librarians who help the public use them. As information systems become more like expert systems, the reference librar-ian would focus more on "maintaining" the operation of the electronic system, and less on qualitative discussion of the patron's information needs.

An alternate scenario for professional identity in a technological future would be for librarians to argue that automated systems, assuming they are preferable, *free* librarians to do their "real work." Rather than reducing pro-fessional expertise to the status of informed users of a computer system, the growth of information technology could create new opportunities for librar-ians to redefine and refocus their service to patrons in ways that show cre-ativity and qualitative judgment. What is this "real work" of the librarian? We have historical examples of periods of creative growth in the librarian's mis-sion: the period after World War I when adult education was adopted as a new initiative of libraries[18] or the period during the early seventies when libraries experimented with many new community services.[19] As we shall see in Chapter 3, one of the lessons of library history is that librarians have wide latitude, from a professional standpoint, to define and redefine their profes-sional practice within the bounds of limited resources and general public acceptance.

Certainly, information technology puts librarians at a crossroad in their professional identity. But what do these alternative visions of professional identity have to do with ethics? In terms of professional autonomy and dis-cretionary judgment, the information-technician alternative is decidedly "low status." In low-status professional settings, more resolutions of ethical problems are handled by stipulative rules than by discretion and judgment. In higher-status professional settings, part of professional life is devoted to deliberating on the response to ethical issues. Therefore, at a minimum, the contrasting views of the relationship of librarians to technology imply different kinds of involvement and responsibility for handling ethical issues.

We could go further, however, by showing that the librarian who uses information technology to create new opportunities for qualitatively rich interaction with patrons is having a more direct and morally richer impact on patrons. A demonstration of this claim depends upon a discussion of the moral value of information in a person's life, but intuitively one can see how this is so. When a patron or student merely asks to be referred to an information source, our professional work is done without an involved interaction, but when the patron presents a more general problem of inquiry, when library programs help patrons pursue their reading and information needs in more complex and extended ways, through reading groups, research groups, workshops, seminars, and the like, librarians develop more complex relationships with their public. Something of the individual's personal life and drive is revealed and developed.

In the chapters which follow, we will take two different approaches to finding a moral ideal of librarianship. One involves thinking abstractly and generally about the role that information plays in a person's life. What distinguishes our interest in information from our interest in other sorts of goods? How are the various kinds of information (data, knowledge, expressive communication) related in value to human growth and development? In explicating the value of information we will be looking for the outlines (abstract as they may be) of the "form" of the professional identity of the information professional.

The other approach, taken in chapters 2 and 3, involves a study of the library as a work organization and the history of librarians' efforts to find the "content" of their professional identity in professional practice. We will look at themes in the history of the public library movement in the United States for moments of insight and creativity in the way librarians evolved their professional self-understanding. We will also identify recurring oversights and problems that we feel are suggestive for a contemporary revision of the profession.

This approach may seem somewhat broad for the task of articulating an information ethic for librarians, but it has a specific methodological rationale which is worth articulating in advance and in light of the overview of issues already discussed. The key to our philosophical analysis is a belief that underlying an understanding of librarians' ethics must be a well reasoned narrative account of what a librarian is. That account cannot be given merely by understanding the value of information; if it is to be a basis for an applied professional ethic, it must also cohere with the narrative self-understanding of the profession in the context of its history. Professions are not like elements on the periodic table; they do not have essences that can be described in complete isolation from their practice. So we need an account that reads like the story that a historically situated and well-informed librarian might tell about him or herself. We have developed that account by talking to librarians and by reading what they say in light of their history. On the other hand, we are not writing a history, but grounding a moral ideal of librarianship. So we need to bring an account with narrative "fidelity" into line with a view of the value of information to a human being.

If we are successful in the "foundational" work of the first three chapters, then we should come, in Chapter 4, to a discussion of specific moral issues with a strong vision of the moral ideals of the professional. In a brief concluding chapter we will try to describe this ideal of the information age librarian.

Chapter 1

A Philosophical Understanding of the Moral Value of Information

Each year, millions of people visit libraries to find information and experience their own culture and other cultures through books, videos, art, music, and other media. The patron who leaves with a novel and the patron who leaves with price information on used cars are both getting information that has some value to them. But what sort of value is it? Given the tremendous diversity of information in libraries, can we hope to make general claims about the kind of value that information has to patrons? How can we characterize the common value of information to the academic library user researching within a specialized field of knowledge, to the business person trying to find sales leads, and to the private citizen researching family history or planning a garden or finding storybooks for a child? Our task is this chapter is to give such a characterization, and it is a daunting one. Not only do there seem to be few common denominators to the value that information has to us, but it is also unclear what is distinctive about the library as a source of information. After all, people also get novels from bookstores, financial data from newspapers, and cultural experiences from their communities and the media at large.

Fortunately, our approach to the topic in this chapter allows us to set aside this last problem for the moment. The library is one information provider among many. Our primary goal is to use critical thinking about the nature of information and its role in our experience to argue that it has a general moral value to human beings. Along the way, we will need primers on information theory and ethics. Our strategy is to use these digressions to form the background for a rich characterization of information in human experience, one that ultimately helps us see clearly the specific professional mission of librarians and libraries.

People do not usually talk or write about information's being "morally valuable." If asked, most people will agree that information is useful, perhaps even crucial, to making prudent decisions—but morally valuable? In situations like this, one can usually turn to philosophers, who are often quite willing to talk about things in counterintuitive ways. But this time we get no help from that quarter. Philosophers have a long tradition of extolling the virtue, indeed the necessity, of the pursuit of knowledge and wisdom. Platonic dialogues often digress on a comparison of the lives of the philosophical, who pursue knowledge, and the lives of those who merely value opinion. The philosopher's knowledge and virtue are usually judged superior in a moral sense because of their possession of a *logos*, or account, upon which to ground truths and values. Thus, knowledge and rational explanation have a moral value because they secure a more reliable understanding of values and make their possessor a better example and guide to others. The tradition of Western philosophy replicates and develops Plato's praise for knowledge in many ways,[1] but the discussion is always about the value of knowledge, not the value of information. Further, the dominant model for knowledge was based on the progress that pure reasoning, on the basis of generally known information, can achieve. Until the Renaissance (or late Medieval period), empirical inquiry was subordinate in importance to this more "rationalistic" method of inquiry.

So there is a danger that we have missed our topic; on the one hand, because we have gotten hold of the wrong category ("information" instead of "knowledge"), and on the other, because the moral value of knowledge, and the belief that it liberates humans from prejudice and opens us to our obligations, is so much an article of faith in the West that it hardly needs such lengthy investigation as a chapter in a book. Perhaps the culprit for this confusion is the currency, in contemporary discussions of intellectual culture, of the phrases "information age" and "information culture." Why do people refer more to "information" as the medium of intellectual exchange than to "knowledge"? If we think a bit about what we mean by "information," we might be able to resolve the dissonance between the tradition's vocabulary and the current way of speaking. In the process, we might clarify our immediate object: to assess the moral importance of information.

The shift in terminology is often associated with technological change, but there are other sources as well. Long before the widespread use of microcomputers, there were cryptographers, electronic engineers, and others at work developing a mathematical theory for describing information. To an engineer designing or improving a telephone or broadcast medium, the semantic content of the information is only incidentally relevant. Whether you are communicating a casual conversation, the weather, the position of enemy troops, or scientific discoveries, once the content of the communication is treated as electronic, it makes sense to talk about all content indifferently as information.

Another reason for the currency of the term "information" is the growth of social sciences which treat cultural productions (everything from informal customs and folklife to formal rituals and rigorously defined genres of art) as evidence. While the popular and folk cultures have always influenced mainstream intellectual traditions, they have never been the direct object of study and theoretical reflection that they have become in the twentieth century. The effect of this development is to broaden the idea of "data" to include everything from the latest developments in architecture to themes and motifs in popular television programming.

It is important to recognize that this shift is essentially a "broadening" of the terminology of knowledge and not necessarily a "flattening" of the value of different sources of information. In other words, we can, if we choose, retain all the traditional prejudices against dime store romance novels and still regard them as part of the broad range of evidence for ethnographic study of our culture. As such, they are as much "information" as a Platonic dialogue.

Finally, the application of the term "data" has widened to include not only immediate perceptions and symbolic artifacts such as words, images, and sound, but the ordering of physical objects as well. When scientists talk about "genetic information," they are referring with blithe indifference to both the code they use to refer to sequences of protein in DNA and to the DNA itself. That is why it makes sense today to refer to the reproduction of cells as involving a "transfer of information" through RNA.[2]

The popular shift in usage not only implies a broadening of the term, but also foregrounds an "explosion" of availability in the culture of kinds of meaningful expression that fall short of knowledge or provide something other than new knowledge. More "unprocessed" data and raw information is available, collected, and regularly consulted than formerly. We also apply the term "information" broadly to any novel expression of an idea or any imaginative expression. So, for example, a library with two books explaining the same thing in different ways might be thought of as having more "information" about the subject than a collection with one. It would not make sense to say that the first library's holdings held more "knowledge" about the subject.

This explication only goes a short way toward solving the problem about our topic. If the "information age" is an historically recent phenomenon, we can understand the tradition's relative silence about its moral value. Traditional defenses of the value of reasoning and wisdom do not apply directly when one includes weather reports, contemporary dance, film, folk traditions, and popular music. This is the point at which polemical argumentation about the value of the "information age" begins.

Notable among contemporary information culture disputants is Theodore Roszak, who believes that "information" is an overvalued term in the popular culture and that its popular usage reflects an ignorance about the character of knowledge.[3] In part, the strength of Roszak's argument derives from the fact that the moral value of esoteric knowledge is much clearer and easier to defend than the moral value of information in the broad sense. Of course, this may indicate that we need to revise the traditional view if we want it to apply to information broadly. We will not be arguing that the *Farmer's Almanac* and the *Bhagavad Gita* are of similar value because they both have information in them, but we will arrive at a perspective from which their relative value to an information user can be understood in moral terms. In preparation for that revision, we should clarify the concept of "information" and its relationship to knowledge further so that we are not dependent upon its broad, undifferentiated meaning alone.

Two approaches to the definition of information are especially important for seeing both the integrity of the concept and its moral importance. First, we should look at technical definitions of the term itself, understood with only minimal reference to an actual person's life and interests. Second, we should think about information as it operates in the actual living of a person's life at the end of the twentieth century. Such a background analysis of the nature of information should help focus our attention on the sort of thing we are trying to judge the value of. The next piece of the puzzle will be to review some traditional and contemporary thinking in ethics by providing a primer on ethical thinking, along with some explanation of recent developments in ethics such as feminist and narrative ethics. Librarians writing about professional ethics have made some interesting use of these theories to resolve ethical issues. Finally, we will provide a synthetic account of the moral value of information on the basis of our understanding of what information is and what it means to give a moral appraisal.

Information Itself and In Context

As you go through a typical day, you hear, think about, and relate to others all kinds of information. You might start with your favorite morning radio show, the morning paper, or a conversation with someone on the way to work. Arriving at work, you might sign in, check print mail, voice mail, email, look at a schedule of some kind, view routine reports, handle requests for information, or otherwise consult, exchange, or update some quantity of information. More and more people in the United States spend their entire workday handling and managing information.[4] Even jobs that we do not typically think of as "information intensive," like driving a bus or operating a crane, can be redescribed as essentially information processing activities. The bus driver takes all kinds of information—from traffic, the presence of riders at stops, the timetable of the route—and manages it to produce a specific outcome. As a "master trope" of our time, "information" is a descriptive medium for our ordinary experience of sights, sounds, and symbols alike.

But clear as this usage is, as an object of philosophical study information appears to be neither fish nor fowl. The field of philosophy known as ontology, which tries to explain what kinds of things there are in reality, has a hard time with things like "information." To see this, consider some of the ways in which philosophers have traditionally carved up the world into ideas and objects. "Ideas," for philosophers who still believe there are such things, are abstract objects that subsist (i.e., they "are what they are") apart from being thought. While the conceptual content of "justice" may vary culturally and historically, the idea of justice "is what it is" whether it is embodied in anyone's society, theory or action, argue some philosophers.

One reason philosophers have traditionally thought of mathematical ideas as "discovered" rather than "invented" is that truths about relationships among mathematical ideas seem to hold regardless of the time of their expression. One might reasonably conclude that the context-independence of mathematical truths presupposes the subsistence of the ideas. To introduce this "Platonic" conception of ideas, philosophy teachers often pose this kind of question to their students: Did the interior angles of a triangle equal 180 degrees before geometry was "discovered"? The more intuitive answer seems to be "yes," and it reinforces the idea that ideas can be "discovered." At least we talk this way, which suggests that we do not think of all ideas as spatially and temporally located (though we talk about "entertaining" an idea or "apprehending" an idea in a specific time and place).

Consider some of the other things we say about ideas: Ideas can be shared and communicated without being diminished. We might say that, unlike unique physical objects, possession of an idea is nonexclusive. Your having an idea does not exclude me from having it. The "same" idea can be expressed or "embodied" in a variety of ways. For example, we can have "images" of justice, just actions, theories of justice, movies about justice, and so on.

Information seems to be an abstract object, but not like ideas in other respects. Like ideas, information seems to be a nonexclusive object. A photocopied page from a book takes all the information from the writing without diminishing its presence in the original. On the other hand, unlike an idea, information does seem to be spatially and temporally located. While it makes sense to talk about "unexpressed ideas" (if you accept the line of thinking in the geometry example), we usually only refer to something as information once it is "encoded" in some way. We say, for example, that we can get good information about the current weather, but it would be odd to say that we had information about the weather, but that it was not expressed anywhere. (Yet no one will second-guess you if you say that you are pursuing the ideal of Justice, even though that ideal remains unexpressed, or if you say you have a good "idea," but cannot express it.) While we seem, as a culture, willing to call almost anything "information," we only do so once it has entered some encoding or processing system.

This is an important point. The traditional conception of "ideas" from the philosophical tradition mostly applied to great (noble and good) abstract objects of reflection (Justice, the Virtues, the forms of things). The encoding or expression in language of such ideas was typically treated by philosophers as something between a minor annoyance and a tragedy.[5] Language, the typical encoding medium of philosophical ideas, was consistently thought of as incidental to the "participation" in the idea through thought. With information, the presence of an encoding system is crucial. The encoding system may be the consciousness of stimuli in a human mind, the chemical process which replicates the genetic code of DNA through mitosis, the electronic transmission of data across a computer network, or the old-fashioned recording of marks on a page. We even talk about the "same" information being expressed in different forms, but we never think about information outside of or apart from a coding system. Information, then, seems to be a sort of "encoded idea" in a system of expression.

At this point we are in a good position to draw some conclusions about how the word information should be used, and how the contemporary understanding of the term stands in relation to more traditional terminology. Data, information, knowledge, cultural works, and wisdom can be thought of as referring to distinct objects of thought which vary by their level of organization.[6] So-called "raw"[7] data, like measurements from a thermometer, have a relatively low level of organization. Judgments, in which we predicate one thing upon another, have a higher organization. Simple judgments about the world or events are the sorts of communication to which we ordinarily apply the word "information." Knowledge is more than a collection of such judgments; it is a highly organized and validated system of information. Knowledge and cultural productions, especially those forms of knowledge that are thoroughly interrelated and those cultural artifacts that are highly symbolic, are among the most organized information structures in human thought. Wisdom and insight can be thought of as the most highly distilled organizations of thought in human experience. We could represent these relationships as follows:

The Hierarchy of Information

Wisdom

Cultural Productions:
Knowledge and the Arts

Judgments of Experience

Information

Data

Increasing Organization   Increasing "Compactness" and
and Complexity   Reliance on Background Theories

Perhaps it is odd to include categories like "cultural productions" and "wisdom" in a graphic representation of information. The tendency in technological discussions of information is to focus on discrete information structures with relatively unambiguous interpretations. But there are at least two good justifications for this approach. First, our schema is based on the degree of organization of the information. Everyone readily agrees that a formula in physics organizes and integrates a vast amount of data within a structured body of knowledge. But it seems equally clear that a piece of cultural knowledge, like the knowledge, practice, and theory of Impressionist painting or the political slogan "All men are created equal,"[8] integrates, if less precisely, a great deal of cultural experience. Controversies about whether such cultural production constitutes knowledge are, for interesting reasons, beside the point. Viewed as information structures, they take their place along with $E=mc^2$. The other justification for including them is that, when we turn to thinking about information in context and its value to library patrons, we need to have a theoretical characterization of information that makes sense of the diverse kinds of information in libraries.

One such theory is the mathematical theory of information, developed by Claude Shannon after World War II. Shannon's views are both crucial to theoretical reflection on the nature of information and yet baffling and tantalizing to theoreticians trying to develop a practical, critical view of the nature of information. The theory's elegance lies in its mathematical character, which seems to hold a genuine insight about information. Yet because of its abstractness, few writers have tried to make the theory's insights practical. Shannon's 1948 essay "A Mathematical Theory of Information" virtually founded the field of information science. It grew out of the author's experience as a wartime cryptographer and reflects an emphasis on the need for the secure transmission of information and ideas.

The key concept in Shannon's theory is the characterization of information as the resolution of uncertainty. Communications which resolve little uncertainty have "less" information than communications which resolve greater uncertainty. After a brief introduction to the mathematical direction this characterization takes, we will develop an interpretation of the theory for our reflections on the moral value of information.

Intuitively, it makes sense to say that when someone tells you something you already know, they are not conveying as much information in their message as when you hear something new. The mathematical theory of information gives this intuition more precise formulation by trying to quantify the amount of information in a communication after taking into account entropy and redundancy. The more predictable the content of a communication, the greater the redundancy and the lower the quantity of information. Less predictable communications are entropic and have more information.

The best way to make the jump to the mathematical aspect of the theory is to think of a quantity of information as the average number of yes/no questions you would need to ask to get the information. In simple cases, like finding out the sex of a newborn, one question will usually do the job. If you want to know the sex and eye color (for this example, assume there are only two eye colors, blue and brown, and that each is equally likely), you will need, on average, two questions. Since yes/no questions are an analogue for binary counting, we could say that there is 1 bit of information in the first example and 2 in the second. We need not be concerned with the mathematical formula for expressing the relationship between the number of possible outcomes of a communication event and the amount of information in that communication, but it should be clear from these examples that as the number of possibilities increases, the amount of information increases.

On the other hand, the more structure there is in a communication, the more it draws on and is connected to a larger framework of information, the less information it contains. Information theorists focus on the predictability of the information, or its relative redundancy, as the measure of this variable. In our example above, we considered cases in which there were equally probable outcomes. Of course, with some knowledge of a couple's family history, a good geneticist can "handicap" the probable outcomes of some heritable traits. It takes the geneticist fewer yes/no questions, on average, to determine the presence of some heritable traits in a newborn.

The highly abstract characterization of information needed for work in electrical engineering is, for all its technical clarity, far removed from the intuitive grasp we have of information in our daily lives. But we can bring these theoretical concepts to bear on our intuitions in several interesting ways.

First, we can see the language of the "information age" less as the abandonment of a more traditional conception of knowledge, and more as the expansion of the picture we have of how knowledge and other information form a process of intellectual and affective experience. In other words, information is always part of the formative experience of an individual in the context of their culture. As a kind of information, knowledge is obviously formative. But it would be a mistake to stay within the classical model which valorizes knowledge exclusively over other information experiences, such as art or the acquisition of data, because we would miss the point, brought to the foreground in information theory, that all of our meaningful experiences have the potential to shape us by resolving uncertainty. If we put the need for information in the context of an actual person's experience, we will see both the value and limitations of the theoretical account.

Claude Shannon's theory also does justice to our ordinary intuition that the same string of characters, or segment of sound, can have different quantities of information to different recipients or interpreters. The quantity of information in a message is relative to the amount of uncertainty it resolves. Thus, a well informed person is likely to experience more redundancy in a news broadcast than a poorly informed person. The "relativity" of information to the observer makes the theory quite powerful in describing our ordinary experience of information. Minimally, it shakes us out of a commonplace prejudice that the information content of a communication resides purely in the "message" and not in the context of exchange or relative to the identity of the sender and receiver.

Beyond that, it explains how we can think of highly compressed expressions, like "All men are created equal" or the golden rule or other expressions of wisdom, as containing a great deal of information in one sense and yet very little in another. Wise sayings use very few words. But "a word to the wise will suffice" because the saying is part of a highly structured understanding. To a child acquiring an understanding of the world, simple experiences hold more news than they would to an adult, for whom the same experience is subsumed in a larger structure of information.

One of the distinctive features of a library is that it structures information to mirror the progression of development in our own thinking and structuring of information. To see this parallel, as well as some limitations in the standard theory of information, consider the experience of a library patron. A trip to the library may include a wide range of motivations: a specific need for a discrete piece of information, a general curiosity about new holdings, a desire to find another book in the same genre or tradition as a previously read book, an interest in a form of cultural expression, such as art, dance, film, theater, or religion. Many of these reasons for using a library can be described in terms of the resolution of uncertainty. Libraries are places that provide entropic information experiences for the purpose of resolving uncertainty.

But do we only look to libraries for entropic information? And is the goal of that entropy always to be the resolution of uncertainty? Part of what we value in the organization of the library is the ability to find "more of the same," to structure an information experience with a controlled amount of redundancy. We might want the same author, another installment in a series, another book arguing for the same point of view as the last one. The same system of cataloguing that allows people to find new and different information, also helps a patron avoid entropy. After all, if entropic communication were the goal of all our library experiences, the best catalogue would be a purely random arrangement of the holdings. At least such an arrangement would make the experience least predictable.

Libraries are also places that allow us to "practice a paradigm," to repeat experiences with a controlled amount of variation and newness. In our experience of information we look for both surprises and reinforcement of what we already know and value. The mathematical theory of information treats redundancy as the absence of information. While that may be technically accurate within the theory, our experience of redundancy or repetition often has a value. Specifically, redundancy allows us to represent the organizational structure of knowledge in the classification system of the library collection.

By characterizing information as the "resolution of uncertainty," Shannon's model may fail to capture another aspect of our experience of information. We do not always consume information to settle uncertainty or to experience redundancy. Sometimes we look for informative experiences that will unsettle our prejudices, shake up our beliefs and force us to become less complacent about a topic, issue, or some aspect of our experience. While this may not be the norm, it is a philosophical virtue with a long standing in intellectual history. Of course, even philosophers usually think of the promotion of doubt and uncertainty as a stage toward a greater certainty or account of experience, but many people do seek entropic information experiences for their own sake. Doing so may be thought of as promoting a general virtue of open mindedness and flexibility in one's thinking.

Our starting point for this inquiry was an effort to resolve some ambiguities in the way we use terminology—*information*, *data*, *knowledge*—and to understand the relationship between contemporary "information age" uses of these terms and traditional views about the value of knowledge and reasoning. We found that the contemporary terminology is so broad that it cannot be the basis for valuing information in general. There is nothing intrinsically valuable about information, as there is about knowledge.[9] In spite of this, the vocabulary of information is more inclusive of our experience and lays the groundwork for a descriptively powerful account of how people use complex information structures like libraries.

But this descriptive vocabulary still leaves us short of our goal of accounting for the moral value of information. It helps to focus our attention on the way in which we seek novel and redundant experiences and the way in which we organize our own experience and the information in a library so as to both increase predictability and to make it easier to have novel or entropic experiences. This way of talking about humans and libraries as information processors accurately captures an important feature of information systems like libraries: they model human cognition in the way they organize and structure future possible experiences. Just as we need to balance, in our experience, the acquisition of new information (entropic experiences) with the structuring of that information (which reduces entropy), so also do libraries have to balance those functions enabling patrons to have rich entropic experience with features that promote predictability and order.

Information theory shows us how this balance is part of the nature of information, because the possibility of the meaningfulness of communication depends upon avoiding the extremes of complete redundancy and complete unpredictability. While the theory is too abstract to apply directly to our experience of information, it holds some insight regarding the relativity of information to the knower, and captures our experience of relatively rich and poor information environments. In spite of its bias toward seeing information as the reduction of uncertainty, the vocabulary of the theory is flexible enough to describe information experiences in which we seek entropy for its own sake.

Knowing something about the nature of information, we can now turn to a review of ethical theory. After this primer, we will be able to give a synthetic account of the role that information plays in the moral development of the individual, especially in fostering self-realization and autonomy.

Ethical Theories

An ethical theory can try to do several things. (1) It can give an account of what we mean when we use moral terms like "good," "duty," or "right"; it can (2) suggest a decision process for discerning the right thing to do in particular cases; or it can (3) give an analysis of the actual context of moral decision making, perhaps by showing how our thinking about moral ideals goes together with a more general account of human development or well-being.

The first aim can be thought of as fundamental or foundational if the theory makes a claim about the "real" nature of moral goodness, but the aim can also be accomplished by merely explaining what a precise and consistent use of moral language involves if that use is to fit with our general intuitions of what moral goodness is. For example, we can sharpen our understanding of duty by distinguishing the kinds of duty and their logical relationship to other concepts like obligation and rationality. An ethical theory which explains, for example, why the idea of duty is compelling for rational beings like humans might satisfy the first aim.

Most students of ethics initially seem to expect an ethical theory to give them a "decision procedure" (if not the actual outcomes of the procedure) which they can apply to many cases. Utilitarianism, which is based on the principle that one ought to act so as to promote the greatest good (usually, happiness) for the greatest number of people, seems to imply an obvious decision procedure in which we would calculate the "good consequences" for various actions and choose the one which maximizes good or happiness. Other ethical theories are less readily convertible into decision procedures. Instead, they focus individuals on specific principles or priorities which are regarded as primary. For instance, a "virtue" theory of ethics might not have a formula or formal procedure for making morally good decisions, but might focus us on specific virtues (e.g., justice, moderation, courage, wisdom) and help us discern how a proposed course of action promotes or exemplifies these virtues. We could also ask the question the other way: Would a virtuous person commit themselves to the proposed course of action?

Finally, some ethical theories take us closer to the actual context of ethical deliberation by including a richer account of human psychology or the social reality of a particular situation. Theories which do this might be called "applied" as opposed to "ideal." Much applied ethical theory takes the form of giving theoretical accounts of specific aspects of ethical experience, like respect, autonomy, or liberty, or specific ethical contexts like professional ethics, medical ethics, or business ethics. Another way to get closer to the context of actual ethical deliberation is to offer theoretical reflection which "corrects" a bias in previous theories. Feminist ethics began this way, by pointing out on the basis of qualitative research that men and women have different approaches to solving moral conflicts and different ways of understanding moral concepts like justice.

Given this great variety of aims, it should not be a surprise that no one ethical theory can do all of these things well. We do not come to the study of ethics the way we come to the study of physics. For better or worse, there is no dominant and verifiable ethical theory to ground the application of moral language to our everyday lives as physics grounds engineering. What we can do is recognize the need to have intellectual tools—conceptual clarity, information about human development and psychology, familiarity with procedures for assuring ethical outcomes, and the interpretive skill that comes from trying to apply wisdom and insight to our experience.

Since different ethical theories emphasize different aspects of human action, we can usefully organize ethical theories by distinguishing three major features of human actions: the motivations or grounds of an action, the actor or agent doing the action, and the outcomes or consequences of the action. The first focus, on motivations, is a little more obscure than the others. It refers not only to the conscious intentions of the agent and how what we "meant" to do affects moral appraisal and justification, but also to the "rational basis" of the action. When we emphasize the rational basis of an action, we are sometimes asking, "What understanding of the nature of human being and the basis of human relationships is presumed in the action prior to acting?" This last qualification will become clearer after we explain the other two foci.

Theories which emphasize the actor or agent take the effect of our actions on ourselves to be the defining mark of the moral character of the action. Character or virtue ethics, which is based on the principle that we ought to act so as to promote the cultivation of an ideal set of character traits or virtues in ourselves through our action, is an example of the type. A possible criticism or misinterpretation of character ethics is that it is self-centered or inordinately concerned with the agent's own development. To this virtue ethicists have a strong reply: If you think about the way virtues and character are learned, you will agree that the best way to promote "civic virtue" may be to cultivate it in yourself and honor others who do so. There is more to say about the theory, but for now our interest is to show it as an example of an ethical theory which focuses on the effect of ethical action on the agent.

Other ethical theories focus on the outcomes or consequences of our actions for others' well-being. These theories are called "consequentialist." We have already introduced the main example of such a theory—utilitarianism. Both character ethics (at least the version we get from Aristotle) and utilitarianism begin from the same basic intuition: Human happiness is the greatest good and highest goal of human being. Everything we do is done in order to achieve it. The theoretical difference between character ethics and consequentialist ethics can be thought of as a difference between two strategies for realizing human happiness: The character ethicist thinks we ought to promote our happiness by acquiring the sort of character that, given our nature, will most likely lead to a happy life. The utilitarian thinks we ought to secure happiness more directly, by obligating ourselves to promote "the greatest good for the greatest number." We need to say more about each of these theories, but first we should give an initial account of theories which focus on the motivations for action, in order to see their distinctive features.

Some very ordinary intuitions underlie ethical theories based on motivations or grounds of action. Sometimes people act in ways that produce harmful consequences that they in no way intended. If we always judged the morality of an action by its consequences, we would blame people for bringing about harm regardless of their intentions. When we refrain from blaming them, it may be because we feel that the quality of the motivation is, sometimes, "what counts" morally. In other cases, we might show respect for others by not invading their privacy or interfering with their liberty even though we have reason to think that their conduct will not promote their happiness. Ethical cases involving conflicts between liberty and paternalism, such as pornography or drug and alcohol use, often fit this pattern. Our moral intuition in these cases is often that, given the sort of being that human beings are, we ought not to interfere with them.

When we appeal to human rights, a conception of rationality, or pure intentions, we are basing our moral response on features of a human being that we think deserve consideration prior to any action. Duty ethics, natural rights theory, and social contract theory are all examples of this type of ethical theory.

While more needs to be said about several of the most important examples of each kind of theory, we can summarize our organization of ethical theory in the following way:

Varieties of Ethical Theory by Focus

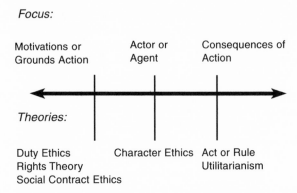

Focus:

| Motivations or Grounds Action | Actor or Agent | Consequences of Action |

Theories:

Duty Ethics   Character Ethics   Act or Rule
Rights Theory   Utilitarianism
Social Contract Ethics

After learning more about these theories, and seeing how some of them can be used to clarify the ethical experience of librarians, we will introduce two recent developments in ethics—feminist ethics and narrative ethics—which add to each theory, yet cut across the organizational schema just presented.

Duty ethics directs our attention to the consistency or lack of consistency of our actions with our duty. But how do we come to know our duty? The purest form of duty ethics regards duty as an awareness of what is implied by a compelling obligation. The first thing a compelling obligation seems to imply is self-consistency. It seems intellectually dishonest to say that truth telling is a general obligation and then exempt one's self by lying. In fact, in an interesting way, telling a lie depends upon a world in which people's sincere statements are taken to be true. So some philosophers have argued that lying includes within itself a self-contradictory motive: The success of the lie depends upon an intention to have one's words taken truthfully, yet also upon an intention to deceive.

Not all of our duties can be explicated in such a logically clever way. Also, there are equally clever ways to "escape" from the putative "truth telling duty." I could, for instance, consistently will myself to be an exception to my general intention that people mean what they say. Or, I could describe very specifically the circumstances under which I would will the lie to be believed and then allow, again consistently, that anyone in such circumstances may do the same thing. The point is that consistency alone is too weak a criterion for generating duties.

In order to give "content" to our sense of duty, we have to say something about what a person is, at least insofar as they are rational beings with wills and motives. A better answer to the question "Is it ok to lie?" would focus on the way lying is, if practiced generally, incompatible with leading a rational life. If we presume that people have a rational core to their identity, then the duty to tell the truth involves an obligation to act consistently with the idea of our being as rational.

What are the hallmarks of "being rational"? Here are a few: preferring order over chaos, presuming that there are "reasons" for changes, planning a life, predicting consequences, pursuing strategies for achieving goals, and treating like cases alike. An implication of several of these features, especially the last, is that being rational involves seeing other people who exhibit the same behaviors that I associate with my rationality as rational. Duty ethics typically involves a defense of the principle that one ought to act so as to treat oneself and others in a way consistent with the idea of a rational being. Duty thus prohibits using others as a mere means to my own ends, because doing so denies the other their status as rational beings who are the source of their own planning. Duplicity, deception, and unfair dealing elevate my own interests and ends over others and therefore violate duty.

On the other hand, duty ethicists remain, for the most part, non-consequentialists. Doing my duty only requires that I act consistently with the idea of others as rational beings, not that I act to make others happier. Indirectly, of course, in a world with respect for others' rationality, people are more likely to flourish, but the doing of one's duty need not involve willing others' happiness at all.

What aspects of the librarian's experience does duty ethics speak to? Does duty ethics help us describe the moral character of information? Librarians are involved in many activities which make information accessible to others, and yet they are rarely in a position to judge the outcomes of their activities on the happiness of their patrons or the community at large. So initially, an approach to ethics which helps us think about the ethical character of our action without having to judge the consequences of that action should seem rather appealing. Duty ethics fits well with ethical scenarios in professional ethics in which we justify our conduct because of the "rational basis" of that conduct—its compatibility or furtherance of the idea of order or rational life.

It should be easy to see how libraries and librarians address themselves to many of the "hallmarks" of rational being described above: they help order knowledge and information, provide aids to planning and strategizing, and organize data and knowledge for comparing cases. At the same time, it should also be clear that the information in libraries does not always make people happier. Having more knowledge about something gives you an opportunity to see order in chaos, but also to be overwhelmed, depressed, and filled with anxiety about the enormity of the task of living well. The elegance of duty ethics to librarians' ethics (and professional ethics generally) is that it helps us see how one can be completely dedicated to a moral ideal which, nevertheless, does not commit one to furthering the specific ends of individuals. This is an important aspect of our moral life, one which we also express through the value we place on opportunity, giving individuals independence to make decisions, and honoring an individual's personal autonomy.

Duty ethics also helps us describe the moral importance of information to individuals. We are so used to thinking about the value of information in terms of its effect on outcomes and consequences, that it helps to be reminded of a way of thinking about value that is independent of its specific usefulness. Accordingly, philosophers sometimes distinguish between intrinsic value and extrinsic value. Consequentialists must subscribe to a theory of extrinsic value—to call something good is to mean that it is good for something. Duty, however, is based on the intrinsic value of a good will—acting in accordance with duty is good in itself.

Is information (in the broad sense with which we defined it earlier) intrinsically valuable? Since information always takes the form of discrete encoded symbolic expression, the question seems to force us to say, if we answer "yes," that each or most instances of information are intrinsically valuable. That will turn out to be a hard position to defend. Would anyone really want to argue that each novel, each piece of email, each advertising flyer, each article in every magazine (or even most of these "pieces" of information) are valuable in themselves? The intuition that each human life is deserving of respect and in that sense is intrinsically valuable seems much more solid. On the other hand, we might be similarly reluctant to deny that information has intrinsic value. It is hard to see how we could lead rational lives without information. While information may be an extrinsic good in the sense that it is good for pursuing specific rational life plans, access to information seems to be intrinsically good. Like opportunity, access to information is good in itself, even if the outcomes of that access do not necessarily promote my specific ends.

Rights-based ethical theories make more substantial claims about the nature of the human person than does duty ethics. Instead of talking only about acting in accordance with the features of our rational being, rights theorists try to describe specific faculties or powers of a human agent which are intrinsically valuable to them in the pursuit of their goals as human beings. Reflecting on our nature, it would seem that liberty of expression, movement, association, and belief are crucial values in human pursuits. Some of these freedoms seem to entail other rights, such as the right to be secure in our property.

Of course, some of the rights we claim in contemporary American society are logically most easily traced to the conception of ourselves as rational beings, deserving of respect as such. So, for instance, we require the government to give an accused person information about the charges against them and we recently conferred a "right to counsel"[10] as part of a general right of due process. These are protections against unjustifiable constraints on our liberty, but their general ground or justification has to do with the fact that we are thinking, reasoning beings, for whom respect requires consultation, information, and an opportunity to respond to accusations. If we were only concerned with liberty, and not the rational involvement and understanding of the agent, we might not have developed these rights.

In a rights-based system of ethics, political and moral rights are inferred from a core description of the intrinsically valuable features of a human agent. Every right entails both a claim on others to act or refrain from acting in ways that violate the right and a duty on our part to respect the rights of others. Since rights are based on claims about universal attributes (features of human agents common to all human beings), rights and duties are necessarily reciprocal.

Most people think of rights claims in the context of political rights and rights that form the basis for legal claims against others. But in ethics we are not limited to discussions of political rights. We can argue for the recognition of "moral rights" or "human rights" as well. For instance, while there is no political right to subsistence in the United States many people argue for it as a basic "human right." Likewise, we have a moral claim on others to a minimal level of social respect, but much that counts as disrespect of others is simply too vague or amorphous to claim as a breach of a civil or legal right. In summary then, rights-based ethics builds upon a descriptive account of the human person with respect not only to a person's rationality, but also to their agency—their ability to pursue ends and goals considered crucial to their nature. On the basis of this description, we recognize both a right and duty correlative to it.

Some information scientists have raised the question of whether we have information rights, and their arguments are interesting not only for explicating the idea of a moral right, but for understanding how the moral value of information is to be understood in a rights-based ethical system. In criminal proceedings we say that it is sometimes not enough to give someone a specific right, but that the person must also know or be informed of their right. Analogously, it might make sense to say that some of the general rights we recognize imply a right to have certain kinds of information. For instance, we have a right to expect good faith in the conduct of parties to a sales contract. Through the evolution of the Uniform Commercial Code, state and federal product safety regulation, and court disputes, we now recognize that sellers can often only fulfill their duties in a contract by taking on substantial obligations to inform buyers of the condition and uses of the product. This is a good example of an "information right" that grows out of our right to enter into enforceable agreements.

We do not talk about "information rights" in the context of legal rights because many of them, as in the example above, are parasitic on more traditional rights. But it still may be useful to articulate them as moral rights. Consider some of our well founded moral intuitions. We think that people have a right to compete as equals for positions of advantage in the society (equal opportunity), a right to acquire basic competencies in language and knowledge of the world around them (universal education), and knowledge of their rights and obligations as citizens. These rights to opportunity and education are, in different degrees, the subject of constitutional and statutory protection. From a moral and logical standpoint they entail access to information. What sense does an equal opportunity to compete make without knowledge of where the competition is taking place and what the competitors need to compete? What is the right to public schooling but an information right?[11]

When we take an historical view of things, noticing for example, the recentness of developments in due process law, education law, liability law, and product safety regulation, we can see the growth in many areas of our social life of a way of thinking about rights that takes the way we inform each other to be a crucial component to doing justice to each other. Where we used to treat employment relationships as matters of mutual liberty of persons to join or quit the contract, we now tend to see it as "wrongful dismissal" if a person is not given adequate explanation of the causes of their dismissal. What was once a right about physical liberty now has, for many employees, an "information right" as a component. In many areas of our social life, we similarly have come to recognize that our obligations can only be satisfied if we actively inform others or notify others of various information. A telling indication of this is the frequency with which discussions of moral disputes include a consideration of how and when the parties informed each other of relevant events or other information.

There are several reasons why "information rights" have become crucial components in fulfilling our rights and duties as citizens and fellow human beings. The more easily and cheaply we can communicate with each other, the higher is our expectation that prompt communication is a reasonable demand and a good indicator of respect, sincerity, and good faith.

Second, the more complex consumer products become, the more sense it makes to treat the producer's knowledge of their product and their diligence in communicating it as an indication of their good faith and due care in the commercial contract. This means that, where formerly the exchange of the product involved a "physical transaction," it now includes an essential "informational transaction" as well.

Third, there has been a dramatic increase in "information markets," organized sources of detailed information about not only products but many life choices and experiences. The ability to get information about career choices, schools, places to live, and places to visit; the ability to communicate with other people who share your interests, your vices, or your aspirations; and the general ability to stay informed of developments in all areas of culture—all increase the demands that we place on ourselves to be informed. The growth of "information markets" does not imply an information right, but it helps explain the heightened duty that many people feel to stay informed. Some commentators have discussed this phenomenon as "information anxiety"; but that anxiety is itself the outcome of a heightened sense of the importance of being informed to leading a good life.

"Information rights" and "information duties" express the moral value of information in those circumstances in which we feel that others owe us, or we them, an opportunity to become aware of some information. Typically this arises as the result of some relationship that we enter into, such as the commercial relationship of a buyer to a seller or the relationship of a citizen to a government. In these cases, specific obligations and claims arise because of the potential for each party to take advantage of the other in specific ways. The obligations in question are specific claims of justice. But our search in this chapter is broader than this. Does any general obligation of justice underlie or authorize the moral importance of information?

So far we have argued that duty ethics shows us the general relevance of access to information to leading a good life. Rights-based ethics shows us the specific grounds for invoking "information rights," but does it make any sense to go further by arguing that the moral importance of information makes its availability a condition of social justice? Would it make sense to say that a society that had the means to make information widely available through public and academic libraries, but chose not to (perhaps by privatizing access to information), was a less just society?

The work of John Rawls in *A Theory of Justice* provides a theoretical basis for a way of thinking about social ethics by clarifying the meaning of justice. Rawls' major work was originally read in the context of political philosophy, but the ethical thinking underlying it has been influential in recasting some ethical issues as well. Consequently, Rawls political theory of justice has also become a major ethical theory—specifically, an extension of social contract ethics.

Rawls' major original contribution to ethical thought is to think about value, in this case justice, as a "pure procedural" notion. In rights-based ethics we start with a description of the human person in possession of an "ideal" set of rights. This description becomes the external standard against which we judge the justice of any social or political system which sets out to protect human rights. The ideal of justice is traditionally understood apart from the procedures which define or guarantee it. A notorious problem with this approach is that when fundamental disagreements arise over the original description of human rights, there seems to be no process for arbitrating competing views. Rawls argues that we can give an account of justice without saying very much about this ideal "good" at the outset. If we can agree to the procedure under which principles of justice are to be selected, then justice can be defined in terms of the outcomes of that decision procedure.

What process would people agree, on reflection, to follow in order to derive principles of justice? Here Rawls draws on the social contract tradition (which he both furthers and alters) by suggesting that we imagine we are writing an "original contract" with other members of our society, and that this contract will specify basic principles of justice. Unlike the social contract tradition of the seventeenth and eighteenth centuries, Rawls does not assume that the formulators of the contract already know what rights they possess "naturally"; rather, he believes that he can specify a procedure which, if followed, will produce agreement about basic principles of justice.

A crucial condition of the deliberative process is that the contractors do not know much about their actual position in the society they are creating. They think about justice behind a "veil of ignorance." They are ignorant, for instance, of their fortune in the receipt of intelligence and natural talents. For that matter, they are ignorant of the actual preferences that people in the society will have for one sort of talent over another. Likewise, they do not know what sort of family they will be born into, what misfortunes they will suffer, or whether they will be a member of a relatively well accepted or reviled subgroup. They do know what it is like to be human, to want good things, and to want to realize some conception of happiness. Rawls' basic question is: What principles of justice would people choose under these circumstances?

When the problem of justice is put this way it is easy to see its sources in both duty ethics and rights ethics. The "veil of ignorance" is meant to focus the contractors on universal rather than subjective conceptions of the good. A basic assumption of this focus is that it is our universal rational nature, and not our specific subjective preferences, that are deserving of respect and protection through principles of justice. Also, while Rawls does not begin with a catalog of natural rights, he clearly believes that parties to the contract will come to terms—that is, as in natural rights theory, the same principles of justice are likely to be seen by all contractors.

What principles of justice would be chosen if this procedure were followed? The following principles address equality and inequality, the two traditional issues in any theory of justice:

> [1] Each person is to have an equal right to the most extensive total system of equal basic liberties compatible with a similar system of liberty for all.
> [2] Social and economic inequalities are to be arranged so that they are both:
>> a. reasonably expected to be to everyone's advantage, and
>> b. attached to positions and offices open to all.[12]

Much of Rawls' work, and subsequent commentary on it, is designed to show that in the hypothetical contract scenario, people constrained by the veil of ignorance would indeed make this selection of principles. Even in our very brief presentation of Rawls' theory we need to acknowledge some of the assumptions about human psychology and values at work in the outcome he argues for. We have to remember, for instance, that the contractors have a sense of what the "primary goods" are in human society (e.g., liberty, opportunity, wealth, income, and self-respect) and that, the world and humans being what they are, some of these goods are likely to be scarce or fragile. Also, Rawls believes that the contractors will gravitate toward a fairly cautious principle of risk. They speculate about the worst situation that they could find themselves in (if, for instance, they wind up being an untalented member of a disliked group) and choose principles which assure an acceptable life prospect in that scenario.

What, if anything, does Rawls' theory of justice have to do with understanding the moral value of information, much less the information ethics of professional librarians? Pete Giacoma makes an interesting use of Rawls' theory in *The Fee or Free Decision: Legal, Economic, Political and Ethical Perspectives for Public Libraries*. He argues persuasively that guaranteeing equal opportunity and promoting the primary good of self-respect would require parties to the contract to endorse free access to both knowledge and other cultural productions. As Rawls himself recognized,[13] promoting equal opportunity meaningfully sometimes requires that we "redress" deficits in citizens' natural abilities by devoting extra effort to cultivating their talents. Only by doing so can we assure ourselves that nonmeritorious factors do not exclude a competitor from some scarce opportunity. As Giacoma points out, free public libraries can be seen as part of such a redistributive system of resources. His most direct example of this is adult literacy training, which libraries have championed in this century.[14] In general, however, one can argue that good libraries "level the playing field" of social competition by negating special advantages that people enjoy by unequal access to information.

One of Rawls' more original claims is that the parties to the original social contract would hold "self-respect" as a primary good (indeed, "perhaps the most important primary good"[15]), alongside such traditional goods as liberty, wealth, and opportunity. His own definition of "self-respect" (that it refers to a sense of one's value and confidence in the worthiness of one's life plan) is so psychological and vague that one wonders in what sense it could be the object of a concern about justice. In spite of its vagueness, self-respect is a concern of justice to the extent that social discrimination undermines confidence in one's self-worth. That confidence is surely influenced by one's material circumstances, but it is also a byproduct of an upbringing rich in sources of imagination, humor, beauty, grace, and a variety of other human "excellences."[16] Giacoma's argument is that free public libraries are justified in offering resources for promoting these excellences as a means of assuring this primary good. Put in Rawlsian terms, it would be "irrational" for the social contractors to value self-respect and then allow for the possibility (on a worst case scenario) that poverty and social disadvantage would deny them access to cultural resources which inculcate such excellences.

These two aspects of Giacoma's argument address, respectively, the two major kinds of information public libraries carry—nonfiction knowledge and fictional works, including cultural artifacts and expressions. What is exciting from our perspective about his use of Rawls is that he gives us a way of thinking about the moral value of information in the broad sense of the term. By making a connection between self-respect and justice, we can begin to think about the moral value of those parts of a library's holdings that do not appeal exclusively to our "rational being" or our practical progress in gaining knowledge and economic advancement.

As we shall see from our discussion of the history of thinking about the American public library movement, traditional justifications of the public library have focused on the practical advantages of making knowledge and information widely available. At times in our history, the very idea of collecting fiction was controversial. But when you think about the conditions of social justice, as Rawls does, and realize that many aspects of our development, not just the acquisition of knowledge, bear on the question of justice, then it becomes plausible to count resources that give us opportunities to experience delight, amusement, and profound emotion among those that promote justice.

The key to this way of thinking about the moral value of cultural experience is to see that moral concepts like "self-respect" are both influenced by our general cultural experiences and, in turn, influence our ability to compete for opportunities in the society. Information is morally important for its practical value in helping us promote our liberty and opportunity through the acquisition of literacy and knowledge, but also for developing our confidence, command of social reality, expressiveness and sensitivity. These are all attributes (some which used to be called "civic virtues") that help determine our own prospects in life and the likelihood that we will do justice to other members of the society.

We have already introduced the main principle in utilitarian thinking: one ought to act so as to promote the greatest good (usually, happiness) for the greatest number of people. Unlike the ethical theories we have been discussing, utilitarians believe that moral goodness can be accounted for by focusing on the consequences for human happiness of our actions. One initially confusing aspect of this theory is that it requires us to think about moral goodness in terms of the promotion of a non–moral good: happiness. This grates against an intuition most people have that "ethical issues" are somehow special and set apart from other questions about prudence or hedonism. In terms of our task, the utilitarian approach seems to involve equating the "moral value" of information with the capacity of information to promote happiness.

What is wrong with thinking about "moral" and "nonmoral" issues on the same basis of comparison—their relative role in promoting human happiness? Mill's challenge is precisely that there is no other standard for thinking about value. For utilitarians, the intuition that "rights" are morally special in some way simply means that you regard their protection as more important, for the promotion of human happiness, than their violation. Given a sufficiently great threat to human happiness, Mill argues, you would justifiably suspend the enforcement of a specific "human right."[17]

Historically, some utilitarians accepted this consequence more readily than others. Jeremy Bentham, for example, was willing to say that the "quantity of pleasure being equal, pushpin is as good as poetry." John Stuart Mill was more inclined to distinguish "higher" from "lower" pleasures, but he tried to make the distinction solely by arguing that people who experience a variety of pleasures are thereby generally qualified to distinguish the higher from the lower.[18] He had every confidence that qualified judges would indeed come to prefer fine poetry over low fiction. Notice that by arguing this way, Mill avoids appealing to a standard outside the subjective judgment of people who experience the various pleasures. Had he made such an appeal, by arguing for instance that there is an objective hierarchy of pleasures, he would have found himself arguing inconsistently that one ought to promote happiness, even if the outcome achieved is not regarded as "happy" by the people affected. If there is an objective hierarchy of pleasures, Mill must believe that it will show up in the tastes of experienced people.

This is a critical issue for applying utilitarianism to our thinking about information. Libraries are constantly faced with collection decisions which pit the public's different interests in high and low culture against one another. Should a librarian buy ten new mystery novels or one new CD-ROM encyclopedia? Should a collection include authoritative critical editions of literary masterpieces, or more popular adaptations? Should a collection policy favor video or print editions of multiple format works? In addition to these collection conundrums, librarians have to consider utilitarian thinking in their reference practices. There are various ways to satisfy a patron's request. Some patrons would be "happier" to have quick access to basic information provided for them with little effort. Others would get a deeper satisfaction from acquiring a new research skill in the process of finding a piece of information. Which view of a patron's happiness is the standard by which to judge good reference service?

Part of the problem in these examples is that we are unsure whether the librarian or the patron should be considered the "qualified judge." Also, there is something arbitrary or artificial about comparing mystery novels to encyclopedias. In both our personal and professional lives we make utility calculations "holistically," by reference to a "complete diet" of pleasures. Perhaps a better way to think about the utilitarian ethic is to say that it requires us to maximize happiness as the outcome of a set of activities or resource allocations. Thus, just as I do not infer from the pleasure of one ice cream cone that fifty would be proportionally more pleasurable, I do not infer from the pleasure I get from an inexpensive paperback that I would be happiest if the library collected only that kind of book.

Another refinement of utilitarian thinking is to distinguish between acts which maximize happiness and rules and policies which maximize happiness. Very often a specific action might bring about greater happiness (for example, satisfying a patron's demand for immediate access to information), but the long term consequences of acting on the rule underlying the action may not maximize happiness. In the long run, you could argue, patrons are better served (their happiness is better maximized) by teaching them information retrieval and evaluation skills rather than satisfying their immediate information needs. A sophisticated utilitarian has to consider the implications of performing the "utility calculus" on both immediate outcomes of specific acts as well as long term outcomes of general rules.

The need for holism and the consideration of short and long term consequences in calculations of utility tell us several important things about the moral value of information for utilitarians. First, we can only know about the utility of information to an individual if we understand something about the profile of the person in the context of their community. Only by reference to the information network an individual already experiences can I begin to maximize the utility of the information I might provide them. Teachers understand this intuitively (and less technically) when they judge the appropriate response to a student by first listening for clues about the student's general academic and life situation. Good teachers often have several possible responses to a student question; they choose their exact reply by thinking about the level of ability, interest, and need in the student. Likewise, we can only judge the moral value of information (i.e., the utility of it) by thinking about the general situation of the audience for that information.

There is nothing particularly radical about the suggestion that "doing right by someone" requires us to understand their particular circumstances. Most people intuitively accept the idea that duty and obligation take different forms in different circumstances. But this is a hard intuition to incorporate into theoretical reflection in ethics, in part because a goal of ethical theory has traditionally been to abstract from context and find the essential characteristics of "moral goodness" or obligation which can be seen in diverse contexts.

Part of what we mean by theoretical knowledge (as opposed to practical knowledge) is a sort of understanding that "sees through" superficial differences or accidents of context. This demand of theory gives ethical theories a "tilt" toward abstraction from the subjective situation of the person. Most theories of justice, for example, focus on abstract rules and principles intended to apply equally to all individuals regardless of their specific identities as members of particular cultures, social groups, or genders.

On the other hand, we have just seen how applying utilitarian ethical theory might require us to make contextual judgments about sets of pleasures which may vary according to contingent circumstances. In this tension between the theoretical articulation of an ethical system and its practical application, we seem to be pulled in two different directions concerning how much or how little the actual identity of the person matters to our ethical deliberations. Since this tension is mirrored in the values that might guide collections and reference policy, we ought to take it seriously as we attempt to understand how diverse ethical theories characterize the moral value of information.

During the past nearly two decades, two majors sources of criticism of traditional ethical theory have emerged precisely over the tension described above. Feminist ethics, focused initially on the work of Carol Gilligan, *In a Different Voice*, and narrative ethics, a more diffuse movement often dated by the 1981 publication of Alasdair MacIntyre's *After Virtue*, both raised questions about the way features of human subjectivity are included or excluded from theoretical accounts of ethics.

Gilligan's initial work focused on the study of narrative accounts which men and women gave of particular ethical situations and of their understanding of the nature of ethics. She found that while men and women both understand ethical concepts like justice in terms of rules and principles which need to apply universally, women were far more likely than men to add another dimension to their ethical reflection: a focus on obligations to care for others and a willingness to give "ethical weight" to particular social relationships. Where men tend to see ethics in terms of negative constraints on their action and in terms of rules and principles that help to define their autonomy or "separateness" from others, women tend to see (in addition to this perspective), another function of values: their use in sustaining relationships and defining concrete obligations to serve others.[19]

Feminist ethics has many implications for the way men and women work together because it suggests that an individual's gender affects not only the kinds of evidence and information attended to in work relationships (especially those involving normative questions), but also the sort of interpretation which differently gendered individuals will give to that evidence.[20] A sensitivity to gender is crucial for realizing a morally exemplary work atmosphere. Also, we need to be aware of gender issues in the history of library work and their impact on current management assumptions and organizational structure.

But what, if anything, does the feminist critique of traditional ethics tell us about the moral value of information? There is the general idea, already noted in connection with utilitarianism, that assessing the impact on others of our actions and obligations requires a sensitivity to context, including the features of context that depend upon gender roles. Certainly, one further implication of this claim is that we might look for bias and distortion in the way differently gendered voices are represented in any information medium sensitive to gender. Traditional concerns about the representation of women's work and influence in canonical literatures and fields of knowledge are an example of a concern about bias and distortion. Given the argument Giacoma makes about the implications of Rawls' views on "self-respect," we can see how considerations of gender might elevate our concerns about the representation of "women's voices" to a concern about justice.

But there is a more subtle and pervasive implication of feminist ethics for our understanding of the moral value of information. We can see it better if we understand the feminist critique of traditional ethics under the broader movement of narrative ethics, of which it is an example. In narrative ethics, a criticism of traditional ethics is advanced by arguing that our understanding of "duties, obligations, and utility" must include a consideration of the self-understanding of the humans who are the immediate objects of ethical reflection. In less technical language, narrative ethics begins with the intuition that in some ways the story that we tell about ourselves is relevant to identifying and analyzing an ethical problem.

The most obvious case in point for an illustration of narrative ethics is, in fact, the different stories about their ethical experience that so many women told Carol Gilligan in the narratives that provided the basis for *In a Different Voice*. But where feminist ethics picks out one variable in our stories about ourselves, gender, a robust narrative ethics looks at the general ways in which an individual's self-understanding leads him or her to construct a description of an ethical problem or issue. In addition to gender, we need to consider (as narrative ethicists) the ways in which ethnicity, social class, and self-image all contribute to one's perception of and response to moral problems. Thus, while there may be some more or less universal considerations in defining moral ideals such as justice, moral outcomes require a consideration of the particular situation and the self-understandings of affected individuals.

What does this general philosophical development in ethics tell us about the moral value of information in libraries? To be useful, information must be structured according to a schema which represents both the intrinsic features of that information and the thinking habits of the users of the information. Differences among ways of organizing information are no more or less arbitrary than the differences among various users' expectations for how the information will be organized. So, for example, the arrangement of the fields of knowledge in the two major cataloguing systems seems quite natural to most people raised in a western European industrial culture. In fact, the further your education proceeds along the traditional sequence from elementary school through graduate school, the more "natural" the arrangement will seem. Both systems follow, for the most part, the divisions of the fields of knowledge as they are organized at universities. Since university faculty and researchers are among the primary contributors to knowledge, it makes some sense to organize collections according to these fields. After all, there is no single system of organization that will suit the diverse ways in which individuals organize and use information.

We can see a parallel between systems of organizing knowledge and traditional ethical systems which articulate normative ideals. Just as the moral value of an ideal of justice can be realized only by informing it with the particular understandings of actual persons, so too the moral value of information can be realized only by bringing the standardized classification system into accord with the library patron's specific self-understanding, life situation, and personal needs.

To achieve this objective of accord, librarians have several strategies: (1) reference services, especially the "reference interview," through which librarians can gain a qualitatively rich understanding of the patron's needs; (2) local cataloging, which allows librarians to develop additional subject headings and appropriate call numbers to let local collections reflect a level of organization appropriate to the needs of local patrons; and (3) public services projects, including educational services, displays and selections of holdings which appeal to the needs and interests of local communities.

But just as the feminist critic of traditional ethics can ask whether traditional philosophers have taken sufficient account of the morally relevant differences to be found in the "differently gendered" moral thinking of various individuals, we can ask whether traditional librarianship, as it is practiced in these strategies, has realized the moral importance of information for its patrons by making the connection to their particular needs. From narrative ethics we can ground a fundamental professional obligation of librarians: the obligation to bridge the gap between the structures of stored information and the self-understanding of the patron and community served by the library.

Several contemporary controversies bear on this issue:

How important is local cataloging? Of the various means of reflecting community needs and interests in the structure of the collection, does local cataloging provide value proportional to its cost?

How in-depth should the reference interview be? This is the single most important opportunity for librarians to take account of the narrative circumstances of the patron. But librarians are split over the extent to which the interview is intrusive or vitally important.

How important are public services in which librarians go beyond staffing a reference service desk and take an active role in determining and responding to a community's information needs? (We will be returning to this issue in our historical discussions in Chapter 3 and when we try to describe the librarian's professional mission in Chapter 5.) In light of our account of the moral value of information, an argument could be made for seeing this kind of professional service as central to a librarian's mission.

Do biases in the two major cataloging systems cause moral harm to patrons? While we acknowledged earlier that there is no ideal cataloging system, we can still ask whether bias in the classification system poses moral harms to patrons.[21]

In this review of major ethical theories, we have had two goals. First, as background and preparation for discussions which follow, it is helpful to have a primer in ethical theory. Second, and more centrally, we have been asking how various moral theories help us understand the moral value of information.

We found, for instance, that duty ethics captures our sense that sometimes fulfilling an obligation to provide information or make it accessible does not necessarily entail assuring the happiness of the patron or even the community. The librarian's duties appear to extend in two directions. First, librarians share with other educators a duty to promote rational inquiry, wonder, and cultural appreciation. Second, they should normally hold access to information to be "intrinsically valuable," because of its general role in pursuing a rational life plan. Part of the ethos of our relationship to information is our sense that, whatever our individual pursuits in life are, to the extent that they are not random information will play a crucial role. The duty of the information specialist is to see, feel, and express in practice the intrinsic relationship between information and the rational life.

From rights-based ethics, we considered the possibility that "information rights" might be conceptually legitimate extensions of other rights that we have, such as the right to legal counsel in criminal proceedings, the right to be informed of charges and evidence against us, due process rights, and education rights. One of the greatest areas of consensus in contemporary rights theory, the idea that we have a right to an equal opportunity to compete for scarce goods, seems to entail the recognition of information rights. While the category "information rights" is not generally recognized in legal thinking, clearly many of the ways we think about contract law and consumer safety regulation express a common moral intuition that "doing justice" in a relationship requires acknowledging a claim by others to be informed in various ways. These "information transactions" are the substance of "information rights."

When we turned to contractarian ethics and the work of John Rawls, we found a broader way to describe the social ethos of information transactions by thinking of them in connection with justice. Many library activities, such as adult literacy programs and children's reading programs, seem, like other forms of education, to provide a form of redistributive justice. By focusing on specifically disadvantaged groups, librarians use information to promote justice. But we also extracted from Rawls' work a subtler and broader sense of the way libraries promote justice. By representing culture, especially diverse cultural expressions, and by guiding patrons from less sophisticated to more sophisticated works, libraries give members of a pluralistic society access to a means of cultivating self-respect. We gain self-respect by seeing our various cultural heritages honored and represented, by seeing the forms of expression we value valued in the collection of the library, and by getting a road map to the cultivation of our tastes and sensibilities. We also acquire moral virtue and wisdom by experiencing other cultures. In both cases, the library plays a crucial role.

Perhaps the most intuitive moral theory is utilitarianism, which reminds us of the inescapable connection between the value we place on things and their ability to promote human happiness. One of the major problems in utilitarian thinking, the problem of establishing standards for discerning the utility of various kinds of goods, has plagued public librarianship from the start. One remedy for this problem within utilitarian thinking is to favor "holistic" standards of evaluation, because they seem to capture more accurately the way we actually think about the utility of various goods. Applying this to information, we drew the conclusion that holism would require a sensitivity to context and an assessment of a local community's information needs and experiences.

Finally, we considered two recent critical movements in ethical theory, feminist ethics and narrative ethics, looking in both cases for implications for understanding the moral value of information. Each of these developments poses a challenge to ethical theory which tries to locate ethical obligation without reference to those local and contingent features of our existence which differentiate us from others. Our gender, social class, historical circumstances, personality, and talents all shape the story we tell about ourselves. This narrative, in turn, determines how we perceive morally charged situations and how we identify and weigh moral considerations. Personal narratives do not by themselves justify specific moral claims, but the advocates of narrative ethics are not claiming that they do. Rather, they argue that it is impossible to respond adequately to others without considering our own and others' self-understanding. "Justice" then turns out to be not only about finding abstract rules by "forgetting" who we are (as Rawls' "original position" requires), but also about applying those rules in settings which makes use of a concrete knowledge of others' life situations.

Narrative ethics held two consequences for our thinking about the moral value of information. First, it suggested that responsible information policy in libraries cannot be developed in abstraction from an understanding of the patron's and community's needs. Like good teachers, librarians have to be more than subject matter (in this case, library science) specialists. Responsible information handling requires in-depth knowledge and anticipation of the audience's modes of understanding.

Second, the moral value of information cannot be understood merely by focusing on the "integrity" of the information itself. Information has to be brought into a concrete relationship with others before it has value, moral or otherwise. This suggests that information professionals must constantly review and rethink the adequacy of the relationship between the collection and the audience, much the way a good teacher constantly reassesses the student's reception of instructional content.

In a technologically rich environment, in which the organization, packaging, and presentation of information is constantly changing, the call to narrative responsibility poses both a challenge and an opportunity. How do we use information technology to personalize the interaction between the client and the information resource? At bottom, the narrative ethicist will argue that the way we answer this kind of question will determine the moral value of the information in question.

Our approach in this chapter has been focused on making a more or less direct application of some standard moral theories to the problem of assessing the moral importance of information. While many moral philosophers do work this way, there is another approach that may usefully supplement the standard one. Instead of trying to make a direct connection between an analysis of major concepts like "duty," "the good," and "justice" and the problem of information, we might try to describe the moral value of information in terms of its ability to further more concrete moral concepts like "self-realization" and "autonomy." This approach, following on the heels of the first one, might bring our thinking about information closer to the actual psychological intuitions we have about why information is important.

Information, Self-Realization, and Autonomy

Aristotle may have been right in arguing that happiness is the ultimate goal of human activity. But the best strategy for achieving it turns out not to be direct pursuit, at least not in every case. Centuries of philosophic thought confirm what most people know intuitively: Some human activities are "self-realizing" or "self-actualizing" because they involve the achievement of some goal or the development of some talent, and it is the goal or talent, rather than the satisfaction we get from it, which is the primary focus of our attention.

The happiness or satisfaction that we get from achieving such a goal depends upon achieving it first. This contrasts with other activities, such as enjoying the company of friends or eating a good meal, in which the pleasure of the activity is roughly contemporaneous with the activity. When we feel pride or happiness after training for and successfully running in a race, our satisfaction has more to do with the achievement of the goal than the activity itself. Indeed, the activity itself, at least in the training stages, may be positively painful.

If people pursued happiness only directly, or as the immediate outcome of an activity, they would not value self-realizing activities. On the other hand, we do ultimately seek happiness from self-realizing activities. Some of the things we value in self-realizing activities include meeting a challenging goal, developing talents we (and others) regard as intrinsically human, overcoming the initial difficulties of the activity, and gaining a kind of discipline which seems to prepare us for a variety of other challenges.

There are several ways to identify self-realizing or self-actualizing activities. One traditional approach is to figure out what the "uniquely human talents" are and then declare the pursuit of them to be "self-actualizing." Philosophers, not surprisingly, have always favored cerebral talents, but none have sought to deny that Olympic contestants have self-actualized in the process of perfecting their human physical abilities. Another approach is to look at the way we differently esteem or value different activities. We are happy *for* people who win lotteries or go on great vacations, but we admire people who graduate from high school and university.

John Elster contrasts self-realizing activities with "consumption activities"[22] and argues that one of the defining marks of self-realizing activities is their unique "utility functions." Consumption activities produce increasing utility (or happiness) up to a certain point (satiation, in the case of a good meal, for instance), and then a declining (even negative) utility. By contrast, self-realization activities often begin with a negative utility (the pain of training, for instance) which turns positive as the talent or goal is achieved. The utility charts below illustrate this:

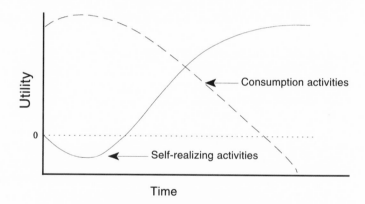

Utility Functions for Self-realizing and
Consumption Activities

While self-realizing activities may eventually result in declining marginal utility, they build on each other in ways that affect their utility functions. For example, we encourage people to develop basic skills, such as literacy, because these skills put higher, more deeply satisfying goals within reach. There is also a "transference effect" among self-realizing activities. The discipline cultivated during one activity often aids indirectly in achieving another.

What does information have to do with self-realization? The most intuitive connection is to see information as an enabling condition for self-actualizing experiences. If I am going to be a mountain climber, I had better get good information about the activity before trying it. There is no denying that information has this kind of value and relationship to self-realizing activities, especially in the information age, when so much information is so accessible on such a wide range of human activities. But it may be that we jump to this connection first because of a prejudice we have about thinking of information in terms of its use-value. Of course information is often useful, but we should pause for a moment before assuming that use-value is the only, or primary, value information has.

Use-values are always hypothetical. If you want to go mountain climbing, then you should get good information about it. Understood this way, the value of the information is always contingent upon the attractiveness (or value) of the activity in the "if" clause. Thinking about information as use-value still gives us a powerful means of describing its importance to self-realization. Since there are hardly any nonrandom human activities for which information is not an enabling condition, we can advocate information seeking as a near universal feature of self-realizing activities.

But there is a deeper, less contingent way to describe the moral value of information. Information has "categorical value," that is, a value to human development in general. When you look at specific human activities one after another—mountain climbing, running, piano playing, studying philosophy—you can ask about the relative importance of information at any particular stage of the activity. But when you think about the task of becoming a mature, developed, self-realized human being, that is, when you think about the importance of information to the general project of self-realization, then you start to see that seeking information is itself a kind of self-realizing activity. And yet it is not just one among many. Since it plays such a crucial role in the achievement of so many self-realizing activities, we should rightly esteem a person for developing a host of information skills, abilities, and attitudes.

When we talk about *seeking information* as a "master-skill" enabling other kinds of self-realization, we mean much more than the simple desire and ability to retrieve a discrete piece of information. The piano student who seeks and processes the advice and criticism of an instructor, the person who looks to literature and philosophy for wisdom, and the person who tries various community service activities to find their "vocation" are all seeking information of various kinds. Even the most ambitious library system is host to only a small fraction of our information exchanges. But our task in this chapter has been to think about the moral value of information in general. And the most general and deepest level on which to describe the value of information seems to be its categorical value in the pursuit of self-realization.

Self-realization is the name we give to a general process of becoming actualized as a human being. But there is another moral dimension of human development from which we can also see the deep value of information seeking. Autonomy, a concept originally borrowed by moral thinkers from political philosophy, is the quality of being able to govern one's self, to make and follow rational rules for one's own behavior. A self-legislating or autonomous person is less susceptible to the control of others, feels bound by obligations which are experienced as his or her own, and is able to evaluate recommendations of others and self-consciously appropriate new rules of conduct and plans of action. Autonomy is both an instance of self-realization and a condition for other sorts of self-realization. It is a challenge to become autonomous, and while we rightly feel some pride at "being our own person," that satisfaction depends upon achieving some degree of autonomy. On the other hand, being a self-regulating, autonomous person seems to be a requirement for other sorts of self-realization. Without an ability to make and follow systematic plans, we could not achieve very much.

What role do our information attitudes and information skills play in cultivating autonomy? In one sense, someone could become autonomous without cultivating information virtues. We all know people who clearly have the ability to form and follow rational plans and regulate their conduct by rules that they appear to have appropriated thoughtfully. Someone could be autonomous in this way yet not be very open to seeking information about alternative ways of planning their conduct. Autonomy and dogmatism are not, after all, mutually exclusive. But the autonomous dogmatist can be criticized as having a less fully realized form of autonomy. Consider the analogous case of a pianist who acquires virtuosity in one style or tradition of music. We rightly praise this person's virtuous self-realization, yet we are equally justified in more highly esteeming others with greater range and depth. The dogmatist may know well and know reflectively his or her approach to self-regulation, but that approach may pale in our judgment when we compare it to the approach of one who, while equally self assured, seems more open to revision, more concerned about counterexamples and alternatives.

While the importance of information virtues is more ambiguous in the case of autonomy than it is with self-realization, the ability to differentiate more or less critical or open-minded versions of autonomy suggests that the way a person incorporates information virtues into their development will affect the way we esteem their achievement. Thus, in addition to looking at the implications of ethical theory for information ethics, we have also seen how information values are implicated in some specific concrete moral virtues like autonomy and self-realization.

Conclusion

Much of the work of this chapter has been devoted to showing how specific moral theories give us insights into the moral value of information.

One of the interesting outcomes of that analysis is that we should now see how discussions of moral value both entail and imply views about information. Moral discourse entails a view about information because talk about values requires us to clarify the nature and limits of our obligations to others. When we do this, we are naturally led to ask how much we need to know about another's situation, goals, and desires to fulfill our responsibility to them.

Also, since ethics is ultimately about the good life, an ethical theory seems to entail some claims about the possibility of knowing of the good life, as well as the terms and conditions on which I can come to know of it. These terms and conditions are largely "information transactions," what in a more technical, philosophical language might be called the "epistemology of ethics." Moral talk also implies an attitude toward information.

When we try to give concrete meaning to moral terms like "opportunity" and "self-respect," we have to imagine a world with a specific sort of access to information. Just as citizens of most countries cannot imagine an "opportunity" oriented society that does not make universal primary and secondary education available, so too, in the coming decades it will be harder and harder to ignore the more fundamental question of the relationship between opportunity and access to information (of which education is but one, albeit major, part). In other words, when we try to live out our moral values, we find that they commit us to particular information practices. Both these entailments and implications show that the way we think about information is intimately connected to the way we think about core moral concepts.

The proximity of questions about the value of information and the pursuit of the good life helps confirm a solution we offered to a problem that confronted us at the outset of this chapter. At the start we were concerned about the legitimacy of focusing on the moral value of information when most philosophical thinking placed primary value on knowledge and rational explanation and said little to nothing about information. In explaining the historical developments which led to the currency of the term "information," we tried to suggest that the best way to think about "information" was as a broadening of the traditional concern for rational reflection. While the information age is often criticized for reducing reasoning to the manipulation of data, in fact the use of the term *information age* seems to broaden and integrate the whole range of data, knowledge, even wisdom with the processes of reasoning that were typically held out in isolation from them. Many contemporary movements of thought in diverse disciplines seem to be urging us to stop trying to value a formal reasoning skill in isolation from its activity in the world.[23] Our ability to describe "information virtues" as thoroughly interrelated with moral discourse suggests a confirmation of the wisdom of this contemporary development.

Chapter 2

Organizational Ethics in Librarianship

Professional education, whether directed to producing lawyers, doctors, librarians, or philosophers, perpetuates an interesting kind of illusion. We often educate professionals as though the organizational structure within which they will eventually work is but a minor and inconsequential circumstance of the exercise of their expertise. It is as though the "professional" were a person whose skills were valuable apart from their integration into a larger organizational structure. Perhaps the illusion is harmless or inevitable; the demands of a specialized education already take so much time, and the fledgling professional will find out soon enough about professional work organizations. Also, the organizational dimension of professional life is hard to anticipate. In any case, a relatively self-aware individual can probably surmise that it is one thing to know one's professional trade and quite another to work in an organization which optimizes or curtails the opportunity to ply that trade.

Fortunately for the rest of us, there are two disciplines which make their object of study organizational life: organizational theory and organizational ethics. The first commands the lion's share of public and academic attention. Books in management theory cover a broad spectrum of sophistication, method, and audience. In addition to the anecdotal and soon-to-be-forgotten management theories which fill the shelves of retail bookstores, there is a careful and thoughtful theoretical literature which seeks to describe the optimal work structures for effectively achieving complex tasks.

Predictably, management theories vary in the way they conceive of their task. Some, typically those which assume applications in industrial and wage labor work, treat measurable outputs, like production and profit, as the variables of greatest interest to the theory. Others regard the maximization of an organization's goals as a more complex and qualitatively rich problem. After all, not all work organizations are in business to make a profit, and even the vast majority that are conceive of their mission in various ways, not all of which relate directly to profit maximization. These broader management theories

57

tend to have more to say about the importance of maintaining the quality of a professional work environment and a commitment to a long range vision of the business enterprise. They also tend to involve more complex conceptions of human nature in the way they theorize the goals and motivations of workers.

The other, less conspicuous discipline, organizational ethics, is a hybrid study of the impact of organizational structure on ethical conduct. Organizational ethics assumes that the way we structure work and the way we manage work will significantly affect both the likelihood of discrete kinds of immoral conduct, as well as the moral commitment of workers to their work. As a field of study, organizational ethics has emerged only since the 1970s after management theory had isolated new and interesting cases of "moral failure"—the failure of individuals to do what they, in hindsight, knew they should have done.[1] Of course, as a problem in ethical theory, moral failure is nothing new.

Traditional ethical theory has, since Aristotle, offered explanations of the causes of "moral failure," usually in terms of the psychology of human choice and conduct. The development and sophistication of moral psychology, social psychology, and industrial psychology gave organizational ethicists new tools to work with in accounting for the way that specific kinds of organizational structure promote or retard moral conduct. At the same time, management theorists were providing more carefully documented case studies of organizational misconduct. These case studies allowed organizational ethicists to track the moral thinking (or lapses thereof) of specific individuals and work groups. Analysis of these cases revealed the powerful effect of organizational dynamics on ethical choice. The immediate goal of organizational ethics as a field of study is to use these new and improved theoretical resources to offer organizations useful concrete advice about how to reduce the likelihood of unethical conduct.

The greater challenge of organizational ethics is to supersede the advice of the organizational theorist by showing that the most effective organizations can (perhaps, must) also be "morally optimized." Clearly, this is a much more ambitious goal than merely suggesting how a specific work process can include more moral safeguards or accountability. A morally optimized organization is one which not only assures its own responsible conduct, but also maximizes opportunities for the personal, moral, and professional growth of its members. Ultimately this requires professionals to take an active role in seeing how their development and the goals of the organization can become coincident.

We will argue in this chapter that the morally optimized library workplace is one in which librarians have self-consciously faced a number of specific questions about the nature and extent of their professional life and autonomy. Some of these questions are:

(1) What does my professional understanding of the place of the library in the larger community tell me about how the library's structure ought to

represent or solicit information from various constituencies (patrons, benefactors, professional organizations, and others)?

(2) What does the nature of my profession tell me about the organizational structures which are appropriate for sharing and evaluating professional experiences with colleagues? Are the goals of library work and the broader values of the profession furthered by peer evaluation, peer supervision, and collaborative management?

(3) How should my professional commitments to information sharing and the value of information be reflected in the way my organization operates and the way in which information is shared within it?

Each of these questions ties a particular part of the librarian's conception of their discipline to a particular issue in organizational structure and management. The intended outcome of this approach to organizational management and ethics is to develop an organizational structure which realizes both the goals of the professional organization in the community and the highest standards of treatment of persons in the organization.

Let us look closely at the relationship between organizational theory and organizational ethics. A "primer" in organizational ethics will help us see library management literature from an ethical perspective and in light of the connection we believe exists between how library work is managed and how it is implicitly conceived. Professionals also articulate their self-image through their professional codes of ethics and various statements of mission. After looking at these codes and statements, we review a variety of organizational models used by libraries, looking primarily for structures which appear to maximize opportunities for personal and professional autonomy. We conclude this chapter with some recommendations for librarians who want to apply an organizational ethics perspective to their workplace structures.

A Primer in Organizational Theory and Organizational Ethics

Since organizational ethics is somewhat parasitic on the disciplines of organizational theory and ordinary ethics, we should first review some of the basic concepts in organizational theory and then show the ethical dimension of that theory.[2] Organizational theory is the study of organizational structure for the purpose of understanding organizational effectiveness. A useful way to distinguish the concerns of such theories is to classify them according to whether they seek a primarily structural account of an organization or whether they take up issues which bear more directly on the management of work.

Structural theories of organizations offer accounts of the possible and practical means of organizing work. Most theorists focus on the organizational chart as a schematic image of the organization of work in an organization, but such charts typically summarize only formal reporting and authority relationships. A theory of the means of organizing work must also describe the flow of work through the organization, the division of expertise and authority in the organization, and the links across divisions which make various kinds of planning possible. General disputes about the value of hierarchy, centralization, participation, shared governance, and worker autonomy are all played out on this most abstract level of analysis.[3] The traditional difference in approaches within organizational theory has been between theories which focus on the characteristics of work and work flow, leading to mechanistic models of organizational structure, and theories which focus on the worker, their motivations and capabilities, leading to a human relations (or, management) model of organizational structure.[4] At a more specific level of structure, theorists study the organization of specific work units on the basis of considerations such as the kinds of expertise that need to be coordinated, information flow to and from the work group, the reliability required from the work group (often borrowing from reliability theory in engineering), and the relationships of various working units to one another.

Management models of the organization start with an emphasis on the interpersonal relationships that various kinds of work require. Systems for reporting, appraisal, accountability, and compliance all have implications for organizational structure but their development must also be informed by a conception of professional expertise and human psychology. This sort of organizational theory has its origin in the industrial psychology experiments known as the "Hawthorne Studies,"[5] which helped scientific management theory become enriched and complicated by a more sophisticated understanding of workers as human beings.

Given the theoretical interests of traditional management theory, the importance of organizational ethics can be explained by the following two-stage argument: First, every management theory presupposes and makes active use of a theory of human nature. The kinds of reporting and compliance procedures a company uses, the method of appraisal a work group uses, and the means by which employees are motivated are not solely the function of the kind of work being done. They are also the result of a view about the kind of interest people take in their jobs, the likelihood that they will abuse their authority or freedom, and the extent to which different means of maintaining order in a workplace can be effective.

All of these views about human beings are value laden and help justify, within ethical theory, various approaches to organizational ethics. For example, ethicists who place a high priority on autonomy and see people as generally self-regulating (when well-informed and possessing real opportunities for choice) are likely to advocate different kinds of social controls to curb unethical behavior than are people who see human nature as corrupt and tending toward the antisocial promotion of self-interest. It follows from this that a good management theory must be grounded in a philosophically credible view of the person and a realistic view of how organizational life affects choice.

As a part of organizational ethics, the impact of management ethics is not terribly difficult to argue for because assumptions about human nature are so close to the surface of our management practices. The second, more difficult, stage of the argument is to see structural organizational theory as having an ethical dimension.

We are accustomed to seeing large organizational decisions about how departments are structured, how job descriptions are written, and how power is distributed in an organization as ethically neutral, voluntary decisions by principles and agents of the organization. When we do bring ethical language to bear on macro-structures and processes of the organization, we usually use the language of justice rather than personal ethics. So, for example, we ask whether due process was followed in a hiring or grievance process. We ask whether a supervisor was fair in allocating opportunities. But we rarely ask whether a specific organizational structure is fundamentally morally harmful. We rarely ask whether the way in which a work group's jobs are divided fails to maximize opportunities for self-responsibility and autonomy.

Again, we might describe a structural feature of our work place as unjust, but the organizational ethicist, in addition to deploying the language of justice, also asks whether the large organizational structures which the organizational theorist describes are ethically optimized for the moral growth of specific employees. The latter is a much more complex question. After all, one can be just in the treatment of an employee and still do them real moral harm.

Perhaps it is easy to see why a concern about the general "moral health" of workers and their workplaces would not easily find a home in organizational theory. With its origins in Taylorism, organizational theory sought to optimize organizational effectiveness. The natural and reasonable attitude that most people (theorists or not) work with is that organizations hire people to work for the goals of the enterprise. The organization does not exist for the benefit and growth of its workers, but to achieve its mission in the society. After all, employers and employees rarely make commitments to each other's well-being beyond those stipulated in the employment contract.

As clear and intuitive as this natural attitude seems to be, and in spite of its grounding in traditional practices, it is coming to be seen as the oversimplified and shortsighted view that it is. Recent prominent writers in business ethics have helped expose the myth that our economic system does not depend upon cooperation and concern for the long term interests of employees.[6] Stakeholder theories of the firm suggest, using both theoretical and empirical arguments, that firms that take a genuine interest in the well-being of their employees are also more effective organizations.[7] Hence, the argument for bringing structural management theory under the purview of organizational ethics may not be far-fetched after all.

The idea that the way we structure hierarchical and power relationships may have implications for the moral well-being of the worker also draws support from organizational psychologists who study the ways in which organizational structure affects psychological health.[8] When we look at organizational misconduct we often find individuals who felt extraordinary psychological pressure to conform to the demands of superiors in a hierarchy. Interestingly, we also find numerous cases of "spontaneous unethical initiative," cases in which a middle manager or supervised employee appears to have interpreted the "real" intentions of his or her superiors in grossly distorted ways. While the evidence is not always clear in this second class of cases, both kinds of misconduct have causal factors in the psychological vicissitudes of hierarchical power relationships.

Organizational ethics has, therefore, a two-fold mission with respect to organizational life. The first is to study and understand, on the level of specific organizational practices, what right conduct demands both of employees and managers. What makes an appraisal system fair? How do we encourage accountability and honesty from managers and employees? What does a respect for privacy require of employers?

The second mission of the organizational ethicist is to study the relationship between the macro-structures of the organization and the ethos of the organization. Since the justification for this second study is less obvious than that for the first, we have taken greater pains to make the connection by showing how large organizational structures can affect the moral climate of a workplace. The crucial link in this connection is moral psychology, which gives us a way of explaining how our developmental and environmental psychology affect moral behavior.

So far we have discussed organizational ethics exclusively in reference to the work organization, taken in isolation. To understand how values come into organizational life, we need, however, to think about the extramural sources for organizational values. In addition to the dominant cultural values which shape our understanding of work, an organization's ethics are influenced by numerous institutions which promulgate rules and regulations that have a normative character.

Judicial decisions, government regulations, conventional business practices, the common law traditions governing commercial transactions and employment, special agreements and covenants between local communities and organizations, all shape the organization's ethical climate. Sometimes the influence is direct, for example, an explicit rule may govern the behavior of institutions using federal funds, but sometimes the effect is more the product of the interaction between the existing organizational ethos and the new, often ambiguous, value. For instance, in the face of social and political pressure to have a policy governing the extension of benefits to domestic partners, some organizations will react by extending benefits, others will react by curtailing existing spousal benefits, and still others will do nothing until and unless required.

The most important sources of extramural values for libraries are the professional ethics promulgated by the library profession through both formal codes of ethics and conferences which support and validate various professional values. Not only do librarians have a strong identification with many core values embodied in their profession's history, but they have a large and active network of professional organizations which promote professional values in various ways.

Our next task in understanding the organizational ethics of librarians is to review current thinking about professional ethics in librarianship, first with a critical eye to the various views and controversies therein, but ultimately with an interest in asking, in the last section of this chapter, how the professional ethics of librarians become (or fail to become) institutionalized in their work organizations.

Professional Ethics for Librarians: Is Professionalization a Moral Good?

As recently as 1961 we can find reference to a history of discussion of the "sterile debate as to whether librarianship is or is not a profession."[9] The reference comes from a librarian, Philip Ennis, writing an introduction to a collection of papers given at a conference on the question of professionalism in librarianship, though presumably not itself an instance of the "sterile debate." He refers explicitly to an argument given ten years earlier by Pierce Butler, that librarianship is not a profession for three important reasons: (1) There are no abstract principles behind library science. (2) Librarianship can be learned too quickly. (3) There is no body of "humanistic" learning behind the profession's practice. Ennis agreed with Butler's conclusion, though not his reasoning.

The surprise that contemporary librarians might feel at the suggestion that librarianship is not a profession may have as much to do with a change in the social context which defines a profession as with the development of librarianship in particular. There was a time when professional status was not conferred merely on the basis of a distinctive and trained field of service or production, but on the basis of a body of knowledge presumed to have reached some maturity and stability; there was a time, for instance, as recently as 200 years ago, when the medical practitioner's claim to professional status was not widely recognized. But this is not true today, and the change should be universally welcome. It is important to allow for the wider and less demanding understanding of professionalism because the legitimate function of a professional association has more to do with the need to share experience and knowledge (whether practical or theoretical) and to conserve a collective identity, by means of professional association, than to consolidate a claim to theoretical knowledge or to boast a long and arduous training period.

The champions of professionalism in librarianship today, people who argue for the importance of cultivating professional identity in graduate school,[10] and for taking more care with the establishment of professional ethics in training,[11] generally appeal to the larger social responsibility that librarians have to promote learning and culture in the society. It is easy to get carried away with such arguments. After all, there is no general theory of the effects of libraries on culture and only anecdotal evidence (though quite a bit of it) of the role that good librarians have had in individuals' lives. The kind of reflection we undertook in Chapter 1 represents an effort to develop theory on the specific moral value of information without making unrealistic claims about the broad effect of librarianship on society.

It is tempting to try to satisfy historical critics of library professionalism like Butler by trying to supply a "stable body of theoretical knowledge," whether humanistic or not, which librarians can call their own. Arguably, the advocates of "science" in library science may have thought they were doing that. But as important as it may be to learn about theories of cataloging or theories of reference services, librarianship, like teaching or medical practice, is closely related to practice. Teachers, librarians, and doctors may each base their professional practice on fields of knowledge with differing degrees of stability and theory, but one can no sooner become a superb librarian by studying only theory than one can become a great doctor without a sense of clinical practice. Thus, professions which have an essential service component will never meet the traditional criteria for a profession.

While it is important to develop theoretical knowledge wherever it exists, it is hardly reasonable to make it the litmus test of professionalism. We expect professionals to have high standards for the expression of their knowledge and the ability to integrate their knowledge in practice with other professionals and clients. In very few areas of human knowledge do we look for stability and the absence of change as a mark of distinction. Quite the opposite. Also, we rightly allow that professional knowledge might be interdisciplinary. The fact that librarians often mix the study of diverse technical and nontechnical fields is hardly a strike against their claim to a profession.

Even if we have different, more pragmatic, reasons for recognizing professions today, there is another basis for questioning the professionalization of librarianship. One could allow that librarians have achieved professional status, but argue that they should disavow it, becoming "deprofessionalized." This interesting line of thinking, which we will follow in some detail below, is not born of a misplaced and outdated self-deprecation (as the historical version might be), but of a sophisticated critique of professionalism and the "costs" to librarians' integrity of gaining the social status of a profession.

The story of this argument begins with the historical explanation of how librarians won professional standing in United States society. In "Portrait in Paradox: Commitment and Ambivalence in American Librarianship, 1876–1976,"[12] Michael Harris exposes what he calls "the darker side of the history of American librarianship" by showing how, time and again, librarians allowed their sense of professional purpose to be dictated to them by the political and cultural agenda of those ruling elites on whose political support they depended.

Librarians initially made somewhat exaggerated claims for their influence on the cultivation of taste and knowledge in their patrons. When predictions of a general enlightenment of the populace fell short, they adapted their rhetoric to echo the more narrow concerns of anti-immigrationists who in the 1890's expressed profound concern about the ability of the country to "americanize" its new citizens.

Librarians took on the role of "americanizers" uncritically, just as they accepted the role of political propagandizer in World War I and remained on the sidelines during the most prominent social and political issues of the early 20th century. They acquiesced to racism in the communities they served, refusing to take a principled stand even in the mistreatment of black librarians until the civil rights movement was well under way. Librarians were generally quite willing to censor materials on political grounds until the late 1930s when, according to Harris, they made an opportunistic reversal of their previous role in light of the popular reaction against censorship and propaganda in the practices of the Axis powers during World War II.[13]

While Harris acknowledges some countertrends to the history he recounts, his general thesis remains that librarians took too many of their cues from external constituencies and spent too little time reflecting on the position required by their own professional value commitments. He ends his article with an impassioned advocacy for a more critical, autonomous development of professional conscience.

William Birdsall takes Harris' story to a different conclusion. Writing in the early 1980s, Birdsall cites some of the then growing literature predicting a revolution in the concept of professional expertise. At that time, many commentators, from Daniel Bell to Alvin Toffler and Peter Drucker, were predicting the emergence of the postindustrial "knowledge worker" whose productivity would be tied more closely to an ability to access and process information than to a background training in a particular area of expertise.

Birdsall identifies a defining characteristic of a profession as the "ability to acquire a monopoly over a specialized body of knowledge" and wonders if there might be some deep antagonism between the librarian's "traditional concern for increasing the client's access to knowledge" and making patrons "self-sufficient,"[14] on the one hand, and the exercise of professional monopoly. He concludes that adapting the "structures of traditional professions would be a retrogressive step in the development of librarianship as it strives to meet the challenge of social change."[15] Professional identity is becoming passé. Librarians should stop pursuing it.

Instead of just arguing that the future of professionalism is bleak or that librarians' ideals do not fit the mold of professional association, one could argue that professions and the conception of expertise that go with them are positively harmful. This is the turn in the argument added by Frederick and Joann Frankena in "The Politics of Expertise." They point out some of the ways in which "expertise" is abused in technical social debates when value oriented social questions are redefined as "technical" problems. Experts tend to polarize social decisionmaking by appealing to the experts' special monopolies of knowledge and interest. The Frankenas claim that when "voluntary experts" become involved in social issues, a values orientation is restored. Given that librarians "belong to a special class of professions that share knowledge with their clients,"[16] and given the harmful effects of professional expertise on society, the Frankenas believe that librarians should opt out of the professional expertise racket: "Librarians are in a position to choose with respect to both their own deprofessionalization and the de-institutionalization of the use of expertise in society."[17]

We should question this line of thinking in several ways, first by asking whether librarians really are in a position to make such a straightforward choice about professionalization, second by asking about the definition of professions as socially approved monopolies, and finally by trying to get a fresh view of the kind of legitimate concern that professional status raises.

Librarians might try to eschew the trappings of professional life in a variety of ways. They could avoid taking positions on major social issues, they could restrict lobbying efforts on legislation having to do with special projects which the government might fund, and they could adopt a lower profile in local politics when arguments need to be made for levies, bonds, or property tax allocations to pay for library services. In other words, they could avoid representing their professional vantage point as a legitimate ground for public persuasion. It is hard to imagine, however, how doing any or all of these things would advance the cause of the "de-institutionalization of the use of expertise in society."

The Frankenas have a good point when they suggest that in an increasingly technological society, expertise tends to move public discussion away from values, but it is naive to suggest that the deprofessionalization of librarianship, the removal of librarians' values from the political discussion, would improve matters. It is simply a fact of political process that discussion proceeds largely on the basis of who "shows up" and what standing they have in the debate. Were librarians to "opt out" of this process, they might become revered as the Amish of the professional world, but they would nonetheless loose their impact.

Commenting on this problem, the authors write, "The experts are no better off than the rest of us in rendering value judgments. When it comes to values, we are all experts."[18] This simply is not true. Discussions of values in a democratic culture do tend to give equal weight to the value preferences of all individuals, but it does not follow from this that on specific issues some people, sometimes people who have expertise, have a unique vantage point which makes their view of the values at issue more insightful and persuasive than others'.

In addition to their technical expertise in social questions affecting the organization of and access to knowledge, librarians have a tremendous opportunity to represent, through their professional experience, a passionate value commitment to knowledge, learning, and culture. When they take positions on matters less directly related to librarianship, such as civil rights issues, they are not representing their professional expertise so much as their general demographic status.[19] But when they give testimony to the importance of a new resource, there is at least a possibility that they are not merely representing their professional self-interest. The reality of political life suggests there is no simple choice to make regarding "deprofessionalization" and the reality of normative experience suggests that sometimes a professional group's experience of values is an important source of information.

Another intriguing part of the argument concerns the suggestion by Birdsall that professions should be thought of as "monopolies" and the related point by the Frankenas that librarians belong to a "special class" of professions which seek to undercut their monopoly by sharing information with their clients. The monopoly of information in professional life goes beyond specific practices like sharing or not sharing information. It finds its most basic expression in the control of the profession over admittance to professional life through degrees and certification. Librarians do have unique professional values, stemming from the goals of their service to clients, but these would not be well served by giving up professional status and relaxing the standards for designating someone a "librarian."

Both authors rightly arouse our suspicions that the monopoly that professional associations enjoy can be used for suspect purposes, but it does not follow from the fact that librarians try to share their expertise with clients (more than, say, dentists do) that librarians should relax their vigilance as gatekeepers to their own profession. As we find better ways to train people to serve library patrons, we should be more insistent that all professional librarians receive that training.

None of the shortcomings of the arguments for "deprofessionalization" discussed here diminish the importance of asking, in a critical spirit, whether a profession is exercising its privileges responsibly. Professional status confers

numerous benefits in our society—better working conditions, respect, autonomy, and a basis for asserting independent judgment. It is not surprising that
groups of workers would seek professional standing. Given this motivation,
we are right to suspect some claimants to be posers and others to be abusers
of their privilege. Harris makes a compelling case for suspecting that librarians have sometimes followed an ignoble path to professional autonomy. As
we look at the evolution and value of librarians' professional codes, we are, in
effect, continuing Harris' inquiry by asking whether librarians have, through
their professional ethics, developed a responsible and useful sense of their professional mission.

Missions, Codes, Guidelines: The American Library Association Code of Ethics and Its Commentators

There is so much confusion about the various ways of expressing moral
values in professional conduct—mission statements, codes of ethics, professional guidelines or policies—that a good beginning on the subject can be
made by making a few simple distinctions.

First, a *mission statement* articulates the aims and aspirations of a profession or organization. Its natural rhetoric is the language of goals and ultimate
hopes. While the tone of a group's mission statement can vary from utopic
grandiloquence to sober realism, it would be surprising not to find some idealism and some use of superlatives in describing the activities of the professionals to which it applies. In other words, you are not likely to see mission
statements which pledge professionals to the "routine and adequate satisfaction of basic client needs."

A *code of ethics* may also state some ideals, but it puts those ideals in the
context of more specific behaviors. One way of doing this is to identify types
of situations that one should respond to with a particular value, or dimensions
of professional practice which should be governed by a particular value or kind
of concern. Codes of ethics also "locate" professional responsibilities in
various ways by articulating the division of responsibility among professionals or between professionals and their clients. Etymologically, the use of the
word "code" suggests a regimentation of rules by category, a codification.
Some professions take this meaning seriously and develop fairly long and complex statements of the specific conduct which each professional value man-
dates. That function is more commonly assumed by policy manuals, for the
good reason that such manuals, being institutionally based, can account
for local variations in practice. A common sense rule of thumb in professional
ethics is that the more specific the guide, the more local its origin should
be.

Professional guidelines or *policy manuals* may originate with a professional association or one of its component groups—either affiliated organizations or special committees and councils of the association. The American Library Association's Intellectual Freedom Committee would be a good example of the latter, while the various state library associations would be an instance of the former. Such guidelines are often modelled by a professional association and then mirrored in a local organization's policy manual.

The most important distinguishing mark of the professional policy document is that it goes beyond the general statement of a value or even its simple meaning in a general context, to detail the meaning of the professional value in light of actual, contemporary professional experience. It makes fine distinctions among cases and suggests procedures and justifications for specific interpretations of values. Where a mission statement might fit on a wallet sized card and a code of ethics might take up several pages, professional guidelines can range from small manuals to multivolume works.

The attempt to define and distinguish these different kinds of documents may give the illusion of a greater uniformity than really exists. In fact, many professions use different phrases to name their unique combinations of mission statements, codes, and guidelines. For instance, lawyers use a book length set of guidelines called "rules of professional conduct"; architects list several pages of "ethical principles" which have the generality of codes. Many codes include lengthy "interpretive statements" which have the effect of model policies, other professions combine "statements of professional responsibility" with codes, canons, and by-laws of professional association.[20]

The point of trying to distinguish different ways of stating professional values is to show the relatively distinct functions of ethical statements which are more or less general, idealistic, or procedural. Most professions would benefit from a full complement of value statements because the process of articulating professional values reveals professional identity, promotes critical thought about the nature of professional life, and helps professionals understand the proper role for professional judgment.

It is also helpful to think about the way in which professional identity is conveyed by different kinds of professional ethics statements. At first glance, people look to the mission statement as the best gauge of professional identity. But interesting and subtle inferences can be made by comparing a variety of documents. We can also look at a historical progression of statements of professional responsibility and ask how changes over time suggest a rethinking of the profession and its social position. We can look at the way professions promulgate specific rules of conduct to infer their actual commitment to their ideals. Finally, we can look at the kinds of sanctions a profession provides for violations of its code. Sometimes this will tell us about the commitment of the profession to its ideals; in other cases, it will reflect the inherent ambiguities of the values at issue.

What does a review of the major codes of ethics used in the American Library Association tell us about the professional ethics of librarians? The first official code of ethics in the ALA took effect in 1939. Major revisions came in 1975, 1981, and 1995. The last two versions are much more similar to one another than either is to the first codes. The differences are so striking that one could reasonably say the 1981 code is the first truly "professional" code of ethics librarians have had.

The 1939 code (see Appendix) could fairly be seen as a quaint collection of platitudes and truisms. Library historian Samuel Rothstein points out that the 1939 code often models universal standards of decency rather than articulating values relevant to actual librarians' concerns. He suggested an interesting test for the vacuity or banality of an item in a code of ethics. State to yourself the opposite of a particular item in the code and ask yourself whether someone would seriously debate the proposition. If your answer is no, then the item is a platitude.[21]

Rothstein's more serious challenge is to ask librarians to state "what they are and what they stand for." This call to articulate mission is satisfied to some degree by the Library Bill of Rights, adopted in 1948. But that document does not say anything directly about what *librarians* are for, only what libraries should do with respect to several specific values. Even the later codes of ethics never really articulate the professional mission of librarians in a comprehensive manner. One of the innovations of the 1995 code was to change the subject term for each item from "librarians" to "we," referring to all members of the ALA, which does not restrict membership to professional librarians. From the committee discussion of the 1995 code, it appears that the intention of the revision was to make the code more inclusive of nonlibrarian staff and trustees.[22] While this goal has merits, it moves the profession yet further away from a statement of the distinctive character of the professional librarian.

A passage of the preamble to the current code and the first item of that code come closest to articulating professional mission. Those passages read as follows:

> ... In a political system grounded in an informed citizenry, we are members of a profession explicitly committed to intellectual freedom and the freedom of access to information. We have a special obligation to ensure the free flow of information and ideas to present and future generations....
> 1. We provide the highest level of service to all library users through appropriate and usefully organized resources; equitable service policies; equitable access; and accurate, unbiased, and courteous responses to all requests.

The "mission-centered" passages of the current code still fall short of answering Rothstein's important question: What is it that librarians do? What is the goal of the profession? The best inference one could make from the quoted material is that while librarians do what they do they protect intellectual freedom and access, and whatever it is they do, they do it well, in an organized way, equitably, accurately, and courteously, without bias. Part of this statement dodges the central question of the librarian's mission, while the other part comes perilously close to flunking Rothstein's test for vacuous expressions of value.

Many items in the 1995 code state important and substantive value commitments to basic freedoms and service. In one respect, it is not even fair to criticize the code for not articulating a mission for librarians, since that is not the job of a code of ethics. However, in the absence of a statement of professional identity which lays out a substantive vision of the value of the profession or its most general goals, the ALA code of ethics reinforces, with one exception, the general popular view of librarianship: Librarians are professionals who collect, organize, and help people find books and other information. The exception, of course, is that while we do that, we will not tolerate censorship, and we will advocate intellectual freedom. As important as that exception is, it is not sufficient as a defining professional value since librarians do not claim that they are professional experts in intellectual freedom or avoiding censorship. Rather, these two desiderata are crucial operating values which are realized alongside the value of service to patrons.

One could respond to this criticism by accepting it. Perhaps librarians are essentially, "professionals who collect, organize, and help people find books and other information." As most working librarians know, taking on these activities as a professional mission will certainly keep you busy. Besides, most patrons think of librarians as "collectors, organizers, and guides" to information. Our view, argued in various ways throughout this book, is that the professional identity of the librarian, while focused on service in professional practice, is more substantially related to an expertise with information and education, especially with the aim of realizing the moral value of information as described in Chapter 1.

Collectors, organizers, and guides can help you find and keep track of things; information experts and educators can help you cull, sift, think through and explore issues and ideas that make a difference to the quality of your life. The "information expert" librarian is not only a good collector, but also someone with professional expertise in judging whether an individual, organization, or community is making sophisticated use of information.

One way to develop this "more substantial" conception of professional identity is to look at other voices in the professional responsibility literature. As early as 1968, Rothstein set out six special areas of expertise to answer the question, "What is the professional expertise of librarians?" Significantly, that expertise is at least as much a matter of the expert judgments librarians can make about information, as it is direct service abilities.[23] In addition, he sets out a list of questions for stimulating thought on professional identity.

For example, Rothstein wonders whether libraries will be made obsolete by technology, whether "we are educators or simply technicians," whether our libraries are "mass" institutions, and whether librarians are meant to execute the policies of laymen or formulate the policies of libraries. He even anticipates an organizational question, asking, on the basis of what the profession is, what the relationship between a library director and his or her staff should be. Are library directors more like "generals" or professional colleagues?

So far we have been exploring a contrast between a "service conception" of the profession, implicit in the current code of ethics (and only complicated in minor ways by the collateral commitment to intellectual freedom and opposition to censorship), and a "mission centered conception" of the profession, in which the general aims and expertise of librarianship are articulated. Moving in this direction naturally focuses attention on two issues: professional development and the obligation of the librarian for the quality and integrity of the information they manage. One of the distinctive new features of the 1995 code is its professional development value:

> 8. We strive for excellence in the profession by maintaining and enhancing our own knowledge and skills, by encouraging the professional development of coworkers, and by fostering the aspirations of potential members of the profession.

Similar calls for standards of professional competence and development have come from library scholars[24] and representatives of international library associations.[25] Writing from a British Library Association perspective, Russell Bowden's list of librarians' professional responsibilities include many of the usual commitments to service and access we find in the ALA code. But reading his account of professional competencies, one sees a much more substantive vision of the librarian as an "information worker," whose service responsibilities can only be met by accepting a prior responsibility for making judgments about the quality of information and its social importance.

Bowden also draws on ideas from a 1974 UNESCO conference which describes information as part of a country's "natural resources" and implicitly casts the librarian in a more active role in promoting its use and actively making the public aware of their rights to information.[26] Some of the phrasing of the British Library Association's code of ethics indicates a more proactive responsibility in this regard.

British librarians have a positive duty to "facilitate the flow of information and ideas and to promote and protect the right of every individual to have free and equal access to sources of information without discrimination and within the limits of the law."[27] One could argue that the ALA code's more general statement, "We uphold the principles of intellectual freedom," goes some way in this direction, but it does not entail a positive duty to inform the public as does the Library Association's code. It is also significant that the Library Association handles intellectual property rights in a minor subordinate phrase ("within the limits of the law"), while the 1995 ALA code included a new separate item: "4. We recognize and respect intellectual property rights."

In other respects, the 1995 ALA code moved away from the guarded, reactive stance toward censorship found in the 1981 code, but it still implies that the mission of the librarian is not located so much in the general promotion of information and knowledge as in a readiness to provide "accurate, unbiased, and courteous responses to all requests."

These may seem like minor differences, but there is a significant difference between thinking about librarians as professional service providers whose background training is sufficient if it can handle the normal requests of most patrons, and thinking about librarians as information workers whose expert judgments about the quality and coherence of various kinds of information ultimately inform their approach to providing patron services.

One could make the same distinction with respect to many teaching fields in a university. It takes, on average, eight years of graduate study to produce a Ph.D. in the humanities. If you looked strictly at the kind of information undergraduates will need from humanities professors to complete their courses, you might decide that a competent professor could be minted in half the time. Even though the extra time spent in graduate school might equip the professor to handle a small additional percentage of student requests, we can argue that a person looking at the problem this way has it backwards: we do not educate professional knowledge workers so they can handle the bulk of their clients' requests, we educate them for competence (or even excellence) in professional judgment in their field. Ultimately, that will produce the highest quality service to clients, even though it may appear "inefficient" since most practitioners will have training far in excess of what most patrons will demand. Of course, there are as many different settings for teaching the humanities as there are for providing library services, so it would be a mistake to overgeneralize the outcome of the argument. But the choice of priorities is nonetheless clear.

Librarians should develop those aspects of their professional codes and mission statements which articulate positive duties to promote the flow of information and knowledge, not just protect and safeguard rights to access. They should make independent professional judgments about a community's information needs, library programming needs, and library education needs. While serving routine information requests of the public is a mainstay of professional activity, "covering the reference desk" should not always take priority over other service goals.

Bringing Organizational and Professional Ethics Together in Librarianship

We are now in a good position to bring the results of Chapter 1 and the first two sections of this chapter together. Our initial goal was to understand something about the content of the library profession, understood generally as "information work." We asked, "Why is information morally important?" and found, among other results, that ethical thinking both presupposed and implied a wide range of information practices. In other words, our information habits are both crucial to becoming ethical agents and to discharging our responsibilities as ethical agents. Central ethical concepts like "respect" and "justice" imply social information practices which librarians are uniquely situated to assure. To the extent that access to information is crucial to becoming a moral person, discharging our moral obligations, and pursuing the good life, we concluded that libraries occupy one of a small number of moral focal points in the life of a community.

We may not want librarians to tell us what we should value or think, but if we understand the moral importance of information, we will want them to see their work as having moral importance. Librarians, especially public librarians, are uniquely situated to ask questions about the quality and flow of information in the community, the ways in which various individuals and groups can further their life projects through access to information, and how the library models the culture of the local community and mirrors the global culture in the local community. The academic librarian has a similarly central role to play in thinking about the information practices of the academy.

This picture of the professional librarian, derived from thinking about the moral importance of information, dovetails with the "mission-centered" aspects of the profession's self-image. As we discussed in the last section, the mission-centered librarian takes on positive duties to inform the public, assess the quality of information in the community, and promote the use of information and knowledge in community deliberations. At some level, most librarians would agree with these statements, though they are ambiguously represented in the American Library Association code. Neither that code nor the Library Bill of Rights goes so far as to mandate proactive concern and judgment by the librarian on the state of a community's or organization's information infrastructure.

In this section, we will focus on organizational models for library work which might realize this vision of the moral mission of the profession. But first we should point out how the stakes in the debate over "service-centered" and "mission-centered" librarianship are being affected by technology.

The service-centered vision of the library professional, while not objectionable in itself, focuses the librarian's mission on collections and materials for library patrons. What could be more natural? Historically, libraries are places where physical information resources are collected and organized. One can even broaden the notion of "resources" and "materials" to include online and electronic resources. But the impact of information technology on libraries does not merely take the shape of providing different kinds of resources to collect. It raises more fundamental questions about who library users are, which of the new needs for resources deserve to be met, and what role the librarian plays in judging the value of different resources.

Not all of these are new concerns, but the new range of possible services opened up by information technology requires librarians to go beyond a service-centered understanding of their professional work. By self-consciously taking on a professional responsibility for making judgments about a community's information practices and needs, librarians will gain a vantage point from which service decisions can be made. This more fundamental standpoint is not the terrain of the value-neutral service librarian. It is the province of a librarian prepared to be a community information expert, willing to make content-rich judgments about the community's information practices, not just about the relatively prudent use of collections budgets.

What kind of organization should the mission-centered librarian work in? Organizational theorists often distinguish between organizational forms better suited to professional workers and those for nonprofessional workers. The crucial distinctions between the two kinds of work are (1) the degree of autonomous judgment required to perform the work; (2) the amount of creativity and self-motivation required to perform the work; and (3) the extent to which the workers and their peers are uniquely situated to evaluate the quality of their work.

If we think of librarianship as a "service-centered" profession which strives primarily to meet patron's needs while upholding a variety of operating values like respect, neutrality, courtesy, and accuracy, then the complexity and professional character of the work is lower than if we think of librarians as professionals who, in addition to serving existing patron needs, assess those needs, assess community needs, and design programs for their community. These kinds of activities require more autonomy and creativity and are harder to evaluate using traditional hierarchical management practices.

The traditional organizational model favored for complex professional work is the Professional Bureaucracy. Mintzberg describes it as the model of work which is most democratic and devolves the most power directly to workers, freeing workers from complex regimens of supervision and demanding more creative and autonomous activity from them.[28] He contrasts the Professional Bureaucracy with forms of organization such the "Machine Bureaucracy" or the "Divisionalized Form" which are suited, in different ways for highly complex and regimented work in which the scope of independent judgment is highly concentrated in specific individuals and the success and efficiency of the organization depends upon most workers' performing predictable tasks at predictable times.

Even professional work organizations require coordination and predictability. Professors, doctors, and even reference librarians must be available to their clients at prescribed times. What distinguishes the professional form of organization from others has more to do with the locus of power and authority to set the terms and conditions of work. To see this, imagine a library with a highly centralized management style, organized along a modified "divisional" form of organization. Suppose there is a division called "technical services" and one called "reference services." In each division, a supervisor unilaterally makes substantive decisions about work rules, standards of service, and the work group's agenda. Supervisors determine the average length of time for reference interactions with patrons and the number of accessions which each technical services librarian must process.

Why is this both a dystopic yet eerily familiar scenario for library organization? It is dystopic because every librarian knows the danger of over-regimenting or micromanaging professional work. Beyond this, there is something suspicious about the justification for concentrating so much judgment in the supervisor's position. The standards for quality reference work, for instance, are immanent to the workers. Reference librarians, by virtue of their training should be in collegial relationship with each other regarding the best ways to serve their clients. It simply does not make sense to take that judgement function away from a professional.

The most profound problem with this library dystopia is, however, that it makes professional librarians purely reactive, whether to patron requests, supervisor's commands, or the latest batch of materials to be cataloged. Presumably other librarians could make interesting, proactive decisions about what to buy, what new programs are needed for the community, or whether specific services are working well. Why should professional peers divide their work in this way?

Fortunately, there probably are no libraries which completely fit the model sketched above. It was presented primarily to show a contrast between two ways of organizing work. But when we have talked to librarians about ethics and the opportunities they have to deliberate and exercise professional judgment, they have described at least some aspects of their workplace in ways that remind us of the dystopia hinted at above. Librarians do, by and large, make a division of labor between technical and reference services. In large public libraries, reference work may be assigned in a way that limits opportunities for deliberation and reflection on ethical issues, or even general quality issues such as service standards or reference resources.

When librarians adapt to scarce resources by cutting innovative public service programs and lengthening the percentage of "desk time" for reference librarians, they may simply be nodding to political pressure to provide those services the public would complain loudest about not receiving. On the other hand, librarians may also favor a service conception of their work because they sincerely believe that that is the core function of the profession. The implications of our argument, however, are that librarians can meet their most profound professional obligations only if they organize their work so that they have time to make complex deliberative judgments about the way information is used in the community as a whole and by their patrons in particular. This requires systematic planning and study of the community's "information infrastructure," not merely a responsiveness to immediate patron requests.

Surely, there is a measure of routine and predictable work in every profession, but librarians do themselves and ultimately their patrons a disservice when they assume an approach to organizing their work which focuses primarily on current patron requests. In mistaking the short term goal of handling numerous patron requests for the long term goal of building better information practices in the community, they shortchange both their patrons and their profession.

Mintzberg's model of Professional Bureaucracy provides a good starting point for thinking about library organization, but it is only a beginning. Since the late 1970s when Mintzberg was writing, a host of developments in organizational theory have taken place. Many of these developments, such as team and participatory management, total quality management (TQM), and "learning organization" management, have had the effect of broadening the range of application of the Professional Bureaucracy model. Many management theorists argue that assembly lines and janitorial services are as susceptible to "professionalized" management as doctors, lawyers, and librarians. The TQM idea, for instance, involves treating workers at every level of professional development as potential "experts."

In reviewing some of these innovations in library management, our goal is to show both the practicality and desirability of these progressive management trends. In looking to these "sources" for library management we can follow the experiences of those who use an enriched professional management model in library organization. After this review, we will return briefly to the question of organizational ethics to ask whether the management practices we are advocating would promote a "morally optimized" workplace, such as we set out to describe.

Sources for Innovative Library Management

A commonplace of organizational thinking is that efficiency is gained through the division of labor. Clearly, no complex organization can let everyone do everyone else's job without risking chaos and incompetence. In a university, some people focus on teaching philosophy, some work in the library. Even within academic departments, some of us specialize in fields and subfields within our discipline. Of course, this kind of division of labor has its own costs, its own chaos. The more completely it is followed, the less aware we might be of the way the specialized work of the divisions is being coordinated.

The response to this circumstance is, of course, bureaucratization. The organization "agrees" in effect that the specialists need to keep specializing undisturbed, while a second layer of professionals, some drawn from their ranks and others hired as "professional managers," meet to discuss the best ways of coordinating each division of workers to produce a coherent product or service.

Bureaucratization brings into play all kinds of interesting group dynamics. Managers are partially vested in the expertise of the professional workers they supervise and partially committed to the interests of their managerial peer group and the centers of power and authority to which that group enjoys access and aspires. Inefficiency can result from managers' overestimating their understanding of the professional group's needs. Nonmanagerial professionals, cut off from planning activities, may lose perspective on their priorities and develop unproductive and negative attitudes toward administrators who they come to see as removed from the primary work of the organization. If bureaucratic managers are also in control of employee appraisal, they can create opportunities for systematically distorted communication as savvy professional workers weigh the relative consequences to their future of correcting their manager's misunderstanding or reinforcing his or her picture of the work group. These are but of few isolated examples of the very complex dynamic that grows up around the bureaucratic divisional structure. The only conclusion to draw at present is that a profession's commitment to a divisional structure should be continually reappraised to determine whether it remains an efficient and beneficial organizing device.

In librarianship and library organization, the most common divisional structure is that between "technical services" and "public services." In surveying public library organizational structures, T.D. Webb found other principles for departmentalization as well: some libraries build departments by territory, clientele, subject area, or form of resource.[29] Still, the distinction between technical and public services is probably the most firmly entrenched division of labor in library organization today.

Michael Gorman has made several interesting arguments against the usefulness of this division in light of emerging technology. First, he points out that most library patrons, most of the "public," rely exclusively on the work of technical services librarians since most patrons do not consult reference librarians when they use the library. Also, he argues, there are pejorative implications to the distinction because it implies that the public services librarians do not have the technical training that technical librarians have and that technical librarians do not serve the public. Both implications are, in general, unfounded.

Gorman advocates the approach taken by the University of Illinois at Urbana-Champaign when they reorganized technical and public services under the headings "General" and "Department Library" services. General services included all services common to library units and not requiring the direct involvement of a trained librarian. Thus, circulation, copy cataloging, binding, order processing, and computer services came under its purview. Original cataloging, reference services and other professional library work was integrated into each "Department Library" unit.[30]

It is not clear that we can make a theoretical claim about whether libraries should have technical and public services departments. Gorman's main points are well taken, but he acknowledges that the technical/public service distinction re-emerged in many Department Library units. This could reflect temperamental or professional training differences among actual librarians in those units. After all, it may still be more efficient to devote full time library positions to cataloging. The real point of opposing the divisional structure between technical and public services has to do with the justification for structuring an entire organization around the distinction, segregating work groups on the basis of the distinction, and creating distinct interests for each work group when budgeting decisions differently affect each division.[31]

Whether it makes sense to continue the distinction between technical and public services, either in job descriptions or in organizational structure, depends upon a variety of variables. How much original cataloging does the organization do? How large is the organization? What are the professional development aspirations of specific employees in the organization? It is doubtful that we can take a general theoretical position on the issue. On the other hand, it is true that changes in cataloging practices and technology make it practical to consider integrating cataloging functions, work groups and even jobs with traditional public service functions. In some cases, it may be more important to put formerly "segregated" workers in closer physical proximity to each other than to redivide their professional responsibilities.

The key questions for any library considering such a reorganization are: What new kinds of communication, cross training, and synergy can you expect from the reorganization? Would the reorganization foster a unity of purpose and mission for the institution? Would it create opportunities for professional development that would enrich the workplace and enhance service to patrons? Does the reorganization position the library for a future in which original cataloging has diminishing importance to the library's mission?

The question of what divisional structures make sense for an organization is itself an issue in several larger management trends affecting thousands of profit and nonprofit organizations. While we cannot provide comprehensive discussions of each of these developments here, we can define a number of innovative management approaches and concepts and discuss them in terms of their potential for optimizing library organization. In surveying library management literature, we found promising evidence of innovation from the following approaches: participatory management, team management, total quality management, benchmarking, matrix organization, and learning organization theory.

The term "participatory management" enjoys less currency today than it did in the 1970s and 1980s when hierarchical, nonparticipatory management was still a focus of management theory. At that time, arguments over the value and wisdom of participatory management made its introduction seem controversial.[32] Part of the resistance to participatory management was a reluctance by managers to share proprietary information and other data, traditionally held as the prerogative of the manager, that workers would need to participate in decisionmaking. Some unions were also initially resistant to participatory management, fearing that it would dilute their influence with workers and that it involved gaining more value from labor for the same compensation. On the other hand, the use of participatory management produced some stunning results for American corporations.[33]

In historical retrospect, the puzzling question seems, however, to be why it took management theorists so long to discover that the people who know the most about how to improve a work process, and the people who were most interested in improving their productivity, were workers themselves. There are various ways of explaining this puzzle, including the hypothesis that a bloated managerial class had come to view workers as lacking intrinsic motivation and pride in their work. The enthusiasm with which many workers greeted the opportunity to improve their workplace was ultimately welcomed, though not initially anticipated.

One of the most common ways of soliciting participation was the organization of "work teams" or "quality circles," group of workers who met occasionally to share ideas about the improvement of their work. "Team management" is, therefore, already implicit in participatory management. But a more developed theory of "team management" involved actually devolving authority upon a work group, not merely asking for their input on managerial issues. Some people still use the term "team" as a slogan, to refer to a group of workers with no more authority or control than they had when they were called the "staff." A more robust and authentic meaning of the term requires more than the occasional printing of t-shirts and bumper stickers. Genuine teams might more properly be referred to as "autonomous work groups" because that less mellifluous term captures the sense of control over work that team management theories ultimately espoused.[34] The goal of team management is to allow work groups to take more group responsibility for the success of their enterprise than they might in traditional hierarchical management models where performance is individually measured.

One assumption underlying team management is that the success of an organization depends upon the effective operation of a system, not just the consistently high performance of an aggregate of individuals. What has come to be called "Total Quality Management" is a comprehensive management philosophy which begins with this insight. While it has its "scientific roots" in the mathematical study of statistical process control, thinkers such as W.

Edwards Deming have joined it to a humanistic understanding of the worker. On the one hand, total quality management involves looking at work systems in order to build the production of quality into the system. Proponents of TQM are opposed, for example to the mass inspection of products or services after their production on the theory that such inspection presumes a lack of knowledge about the quality of the system and, worse still, an acceptance of a work system "out of statistical control." Careful study of variations in quality at every stage of the work system and periodic monitoring of key variables can assure that a work system is "optimized" for a specific quality of goods or services.

From a humanistic perspective, TQM encourages workers to focus on the quality of their work rather than their fear that the individual mistakes they make will result in penalties for them. A TQM work environment consequently requires a weakening of individual performance appraisal systems and the promotion of a genuine feeling of security on the part of workers. One of Deming's 14 points was, "Drive out fear." Underlying his view of the worker was a belief that if workers did not have to fear for the immediate consequences of their mistakes, if workers could candidly identify where they needed retraining or new placement, then they would cooperate in analyzing the work system in a more disinterested way and yet take much more pride in their own workmanship. The fearful worker conceals skill deficits, deflects blame, and poisons the work atmosphere. While Deming can be accused of idealism in his appraisal of the worker's underlying interest in pride in workmanship, there is considerable evidence of workplaces in which TQM has successfully refocused employee attention on the quality of the work system.

It is hard to deny that TQM, especially Deming's version of it, asks a lot from workers. Critics say that professional workers especially want a strong system of individual performance appraisal so they can climb the ranks of their career unimpeded by their less illustrious colleagues. The considerable skepticism of corporations in the United States over the "humanistic" aspect of TQM has led to a more scientific focus for most TQM applications.

It might be helpful to distinguish this narrow version of the theory, we could call it analytic-TQM, from the broader management philosophy that thinkers like Deming tried to develop under the label total quality management. The former involves using a special team of "quality experts" to measure, analyze, diagnose, and offer remedies for a work system's most extreme variations in quality. The latter is a comprehensive management philosophy which begins with probing discussions (carried out by workers) about the "real" mission of the organization, its customers, suppliers, and other constituents. It requires a change in the ethos of the workplace and it assumes a much broader involvement and commitment from all of the employees in the organization.

This latter approach to TQM is the true heir to earlier experimentation with participation and teamwork because it treats the involvement and control of work by teams as crucial to analyzing the work system. While the level of commitment, involvement, and change required for this approach puts it out of reach of most organizations, the most impressive results from using TQM seem to come from organizations which have succeeded in adopting it as a philosophy.[35] In the last section of this chapter, we will discuss the ethical difference that this total quality approach makes.

At its root, either version of total quality management requires detailed and careful measurement of discrete outcomes of the organization's work flow. One technique for evaluating the measurements demanded by the theory is called benchmarking, a practice by which measures of a system and its performance are made comparable to other similar organizations. For instance, when a group of similar academic libraries compare the percentage of the library's budget to the university budget they are creating a benchmark (crude as it is) for assessing the adequacy of their budgets. Total quality management, and other international quality standards such as ISO 9000, have tried to raise "benchmarking" from an ad hoc technique for making policy arguments to a reliable and reputable form of comparative analysis.

Hundreds of academic institutions have tried to apply TQM at their institutions.[36] In 1993, an issue of *Special Libraries* was devoted to discussion of quality management and related issues in special and academic libraries. The useful articles in that collection show how benchmarking and quality management can be applied to information professions.

One of the general values of instituting benchmarking in library work is that it forces librarians out of a passive, patron-driven paradigm of service. Instead of asking whether library staff were "available" for patron needs, the benchmarking process forces a more active measurement of how well the library staff supply the information needs of their customers. While an over-eager benchmarker could try to excessively quantify his or her professional interactions, sensible benchmarking can help librarians focus on their patron's information practices and needs more closely.[37] This may be easier in a special library, such as a library serving a research laboratory, where the relationship between library mission and patron needs is tight and easy to define.

The last two management concepts in our review of innovative management techniques are matrix organization and learning organization. The first refers to a way of rethinking hierarchy by distributing authority for managerial tasks among workers who come to see themselves in a complex matrix of relationships. A traditional "command and control" hierarchy can be thought of as a one-dimensional matrix. Most work processes (supervision, deliberation, and reporting, for instance) are organized along a single vertical axis which represents more or less power and authority. Any delegation of authority outside the traditional hierarchy requires the special commission of a committee or working group.

What if the major managerial functions of the workplace (including coordination functions) were all distributed among staff members? Each staff member would be a partial "boss" of many others and each would be in a reporting relationship with several colleagues. One way to imagine a matrix organization is to see it as an extreme version of what many managers already do when they delegate specific responsibilities (such as scheduling the reference desk or investigating a particular problem) to supervised workers.

If we distributed all of the traditional manager's responsibilities in this way, would we still have managers? We would still have managerial functions, and some of them would have high and low status. For instance, serving as the liaison to the library trustees would have more status than scheduling the reference desk. However, a matrix organization might take steps to avoid consolidation of power in a specific individual's hands. After all, part of the motivation of matrix organization is to distribute power and authority and enhance the flow of information within a work group.

In one sense, the matrix organized staff has as many managers as it does staff members. Each staff member may have as many bosses as well. The matrix approach places a premium on communication, cooperation, and negotiation,[38] since coercive authority is distributed. It also forces us to organize work practically, according to the flow of work, and to reorganize many tasks continually. It promises to reduce the need for committees and managerial overhead by beginning with an integrative principle of work organization, rather than beginning by dividing labor and then reintegrating it in management.

Should librarians have a special interest in matrix organization? As a collegial model of organization, the matrix approach extends Mintzberg's original model of "professional bureaucracy" in useful ways. Matrix organization is well suited to work environments which have fast paced technological change, professional work which requires both autonomy and coordination of resources, and workplaces which need to operate holistically.[39] Beyond this, librarians, as information professionals, might take a special interest in the high demand that matrix organization places on workplace communication systems.

With more broadly distributed authority, the members of a matrix work group have more complex communication needs and must adopt new information practices to satisfy them. Part of the elegance of the old command and control hierarchy was that it was easy to identify the person "in charge." In a matrix system, more people are in charge of more things. The potential for conflict and coordination problems increases with the complexity of the matrix. However, if librarians want to be information professionals not only in the sense that they use sophisticated information resources, but also because they challenge themselves to use sophisticated information work practices, then matrix organization might be appealing.

Like total quality management and participatory management before it, a matrix organization expands opportunities for autonomy and self-directed work. The crucial question for librarians considering this management approach is whether they see themselves as professionals requiring self-directed deliberative control of their work or as professionals whose work can largely be coordinated and directed by managerial professionals.

The "learning organization" is one which has set about optimizing its ability both to carry out its present mission and to "learn" about itself and its environment so that it can adapt quickly to new developments and future trends. The major question this kind of management thought poses for an organization is, How well does the organization learn about itself and its market?

Management experts recommend learning organization skills for work groups experiencing rapid technological change since these skills are particularly designed to move organizations away from an excessive focus on their existing stock of professional knowledge. Learning organizations are by definition oriented toward a future in which professional practice will be different than it has been. There is an interesting irony to librarians' thinking about the importance of learning organization theory since they are in fact professionals devoted to the learning needs of others.

Minimally, the learning organization is one which has implemented professional development for its staff. Thus, the professional development plank (Number 8) of the American Library Association's code of ethics would seem to support the idea of a "learning professional," if not organization. But beyond "encouraging" professionals to develop individual abilities and skills, the learning organization makes the worker's and the institution's development a priority by institutionalizing self-study, market research, and futuristic planning. It seems obvious that librarians have a special professional commitment to making their institutions "learning organizations," yet we suspect many librarians would be hard pressed to explain how their workplace institutionalizes the kind of learning called for by the theory.

Choosing Management Structures Which Optimize Ethics

So far we have been discussing innovative management thinking which enhances the traditional organizational model for professional work. We have paid special attention to theories and concepts which speak to the contemporary climate of change in professional, technology related work. But how does promoting organizational effectiveness in these ways promote ethics? One can imagine a library which is "effective" by some credible measures (good resources are bought and cataloged in a timely fashion, librarians and staff show up on time to do the work they are assigned, highly motivated and competent professional administrators supervise librarians fairly) and yet not a particularly desirable place to work from an ethical standpoint.

But even this thought experiment requires us to smuggle in normative language. What makes the new accessions "good"? Do they further the community's information habits and practices? By what standard? Against what understanding of professional mission are the administrators judged competent? In what sense are they "fair"? Could an organization be effective without treating its workers fairly?

Even though some measures of organizational effectiveness may be more or less removed from immediate ethical implications, our view is that a library cannot be "optimized" for effectiveness without a mission-centered conception of professional identity and value-oriented management philosophy, which ultimately leads to its being ethically optimized as well. Organizational effectiveness is too intricately entwined with questions of mission and presuppositions about the nature of professional obligation to separate the two kinds of questions completely or finally.

What is an ethically optimized organization and how do the management approaches discussed in this chapter promote optimization? We answered the first part of this question earlier in the chapter when we defined a morally optimized organization as "one which not only assures its own responsible conduct, but also maximizes opportunities for the personal and professional growth of its members." In order to answer the second part of the question, we need to briefly describe a model of moral growth against which to judge the management approaches we introduced above.

Applied ethicists and moral psychologists try to describe moral growth in terms of a theory of moral agency, roughly a view about what it means to be a fully developed moral person. This is admittedly a highly interpretive, culturally specific project. On the other hand, some important empirical work has been done in moral psychology and there is some consensus about the broad outlines of moral agency. The most famous empirical contribution to agency theory is Kohlberg's hierarchy of moral development. Kohlberg modelled moral agency in stages of development based on patterns of response from test subjects to a particular moral problem. Each stage in Kohlberg's hierarchy involves a progressively greater realization of the ego independence of moral rules and laws. Morally developed agents are people who, among other things, come to see their interests as comparable to others and who see moral law as grounded in reason and nature, rather than power and self-interest.

The crucial question for us as organizational theorists is, "What environment helps people acquire these features?" Here we should start with deference to one of the first moral psychologists, Aristotle, who argued that habituation, modelling, and life in a well-ordered community were crucial components of moral development. Once we escape the prejudice that moral development is largely complete before we enter the world of work, we are ready to focus on the way our work environment models higher stages of moral development.

In her excellent article, "Infoethics for Leaders: Models of Moral Agency in the Information Environment," Martha Montague Smith integrates some general problems of moral agency with the specific demands of professional life in librarianship.[40] She shows, generally, how moral agency in adults requires an integration of several role-specific and value-specific "selves"—public, private, professional, and personal. Each of these, in turn, has several dimensions and inherent conflicts.

Competing demands from patrons, colleagues, and professional institutions complicate the task of integrating the professional self for librarians. Smith discusses the various kinds of ethical responses that workplaces with different ethical climates elicit. Some work environments position us for "ideal" ethical deliberation in which we can engage in the most profound and probing discussion of our mission and obligations while other workplaces elicit "survival ethics" in which we try "creatively" (though not always ethically) to adapt to the failure of the workplace to address ethical concerns.

Going beyond these predictions of ethical response, we can try to ask which management practices are likely to promote "profound and probing discussion" of the values that guide professional life. The answer, by now, may seem obvious. The ethically optimized workplace is one in which workers are given maximum involvement and control in defining and discharging their professional obligations while at the same time holding themselves to the highest standards of accountability to the larger professional community as it tries to do the same. Only workers who take responsibility for their work and take responsibility for working with others will model the kind of independence of judgment that we associate with fully realized moral agents.

Thus, it is crucially important, but not sufficient, to devolve power to workers. In the absence of controls and checks ("reality checks"), such a strategy may backfire. That is why benchmarking is important. It is also an important feature of matrix organizations that they encourage cooperative behavior so that individuals cannot become "carried away" with their authority or their sense of the importance of the tasks or issues they manage. And, of course, cultivation of "self-responsibility" is central to the TQM orientation toward the customer and the performance of the work system.

On the one hand, the morally optimized workplace empowers workers by focusing them away from narrow authority relationships and personal self-interest and toward the question of the quality of their work. On the other hand, the empowered worker, having been given more control and autonomy, is held accountable to more public and verifiable criteria of success. Management practices which promote both aspects of this model of moral development simultaneously optimize the effectiveness of the organization and the moral growth of its work force.

This approach has an interesting consequence, which points us logically toward the next chapter. In starting this inquiry into ethics for librarians in the information age, we were naturally led to consider the moral value of information, since that is the object of professional library practice. We also had a fairly natural interest in reviewing the profession's self-understanding of mission as it is reflected in its code of ethics and the management practices common to library administration. But to think deeply about the larger social context within which the profession is imbedded, we need to look at several defining issues in professional life in historical context.

The view of the morally self-realized librarian which we have just articulated requires that independent thinking about professional mission be "checked" by consulting the reality of the library's involvement in the larger community. By tracking several key issues in the evolution of the profession in the American public library movement, we propose to add much needed depth to our understanding of the moral values that should guide library work in the information age.

Chapter 3

The Search for a Professional Mission

The study of information theory, ethical theories, and the organizational structures that govern libraries is only part of the larger picture of how libraries and librarians resolve ethical issues. All professions and organizations are shaped and influenced by both the history out of which they have risen and the myths that have grown up around that history. Cultural stereotypes of libraries and librarians are the direct result of historical events and images that have permeated the American consciousness. It is limiting to think that we can discuss ethical decision making without looking at the historical views of the mission of the library and the role of the librarian in developing that mission.

History is not static, and it is also important to see how, as the century progressed, librarians attempted to change both the mission of the library and the role of the librarian. But that changing and redirecting of the mission of American libraries has not been an abandonment but a modification of the traditional library mission.

While librarians may have tried to change the image and mission of the library, the public still clings to the history and stereotypes of the past. The most common view of libraries provided by the media is the stereotypical one of libraries as boring, quiet places full of knowledge and the librarian as the glasses and bun defender of silence and intellectual pursuits. This stereotype, as much as librarians rail against it, is also based on a reality and an ethos that is still a part of the contemporary American library.

Not only the public but also the profession holds on to the myths that have grown up around the history of the American public library. The spirit of public service, the library as an educational institution, and the library as a safe, wholesome and cultural place for the family are all values that still hold sway over the majority of American librarians. While we may debate the issues of "fee or free" or the privatization of library services, those are seen as issues that will affect only a few public libraries, and perhaps some academic and special libraries. They are not viewed as serious threats to our vision of what a public library was meant to be, a place for the free pursuit of knowledge.

While some may reject the study of the past to illuminate the future, the reality is that we cannot escape from our past either as persons or as a profession. The past shapes and molds what we are today. Michael Harris in his article "Why Do We Study Library History?" presents the need for conscious attention to and interpretation of the history of libraries and librarians in all areas of research. According to him, the move to the study of the postindustrial society, the implications of the age of technology, and the move away from the book have for some also meant a move away from past research and the study of traditional book centered libraries.[1] This move not only rejects the past but it does not allow us to see that the decisions we make regarding technology come from the visions and values of the past.

In this chapter we will examine some historical library values and the conflicts that have arisen from them, especially when those values are applied to specific ethical issues. We will also examine the historical mission of the profession and the growth of librarianship from the founding of the American Library Association to the present, and discuss its impact on how librarians make ethical decisions.

Mission of the American Public Library

As the United States entered a new age of libraries and publicly supported access to information, it also entered an age of increased access to other types of printed information. The number of books published doubled from 1880 to 1890 and tripled from 1890 to 1910.[2] The number of newspapers published rose from 254 in 1850 to 2,226 in 1900 with circulation figures rising from 758,000 in 1850 to 15,102,000 in 1900.[3] The library was only one aspect of the rapid change in the role of information that took place a century ago and that is taking place in the current "information age."

The birth of the modern American public library movement has been traditionally dated by the opening of the Boston Public Library in 1854, because that date marks the beginning of a dramatic increase in the public's access to books and information. Like most social and political movements, this one grew out of the vision of a few and became the concern of all. From the beginning, the library movement was developed by individual leaders such as George Ticknor and Melvil Dewey, who had strong personal visions for both libraries and the profession. But while these and the other library leaders had some shared values and organizational goals, there was no shared vision for what libraries should be. This lack of consensus and conflicting motives and agendas for libraries have resulted, after 150 years, in librarians' asking themselves, Why are we here? and How do we make decisions regarding our mission and ethics?

This chapter will focus on how library history can help us attempt to answer those questions. While recognizing that various types of libraries—academic, public, special, and school—have differing histories, we will most often be referring to public library history. While individual libraries may have espoused a variety of purposes and missions, we have chosen to focus our brief look at library history on three common components of the public library mission in the United States at the turn of the century. We will examine these components and try to determine how they have been changed or reinterpreted by revisionist library history and how they are still part of our cultural myths surrounding libraries. And most importantly, we will examine how these aspects of library history affect librarians' ethical decision making today.

These three core components are the library as a place of education, the library as the uplifter of the common person, and the library as cultural center of the community.

Education was always a key element in promoting the public library. The library was seen as the "people's university" and the place where education was available to all. For some this was the only justification for public funds to be used. Josiah Quincy states in "Function of a Town Library" in 1875 that the reason that taxes are endured for the public library is education:

> Upon what principle can the citizen, who thinks before he casts his ballot, justify himself in voting increased taxes upon his neighbors for the purpose of establishing a library? He must assume the necessity of public schools, and then argue that he may vote for a library that will supplement the elementary instruction which the town provides. And the justification is ample. If our schools are so conducted as to awaken a taste for knowledge and give a correct method in English reading the town library may represent the university brought to everyman's door.[4]

Taxation for the sake of knowledge and education was acceptable, and since the public had already agreed to be taxed for public schools, the educational connection between public libraries and public schools was frequently used as justification for the development of the public library. A common theory was that the public school system had planted seeds of knowledge and the thirst for learning in the young, who then needed the public library to continue and nurture their education. Library advocates also argued that public school teachers needed to be able to expand and develop their intellects through the public library.

The emphasis on the library as an educational institution could be seen in many of the developments and programs of public libraries. The establishment of children's reading areas, the work with school libraries and the development of reading and self-improvement programs for factory workers, apprentices, and immigrant populations were common examples of the educational mission. In the 1920s, reading courses were provided by various public libraries and under the direction of reader's-advisor librarians whose job it was to prepare and supervise courses of reading for individual patrons.[5]

The idea that education was an acceptable role for tax-supported libraries also led to the corollary, in the late 1800s, that spending public money on recreational reading was not acceptable. When the first Carnegie library was established in Pittsburgh in 1890, public concern was raised that 70 percent of the book money was to be spent for the purchase of fiction. Citizens questioned why the city was spending that amount of money on pure amusement.[6] This negative view of recreational reading was to change by the beginning of the twentieth century but it influenced librarians and collection development decisions for years to come.

New interpretations of library history view the role of education in a different light. These revisionist library historians still see education as a prime purpose and value but question the motivation of the library leaders of the time. Michael Harris, in his work "Purpose of the American Library in Historical Perspective," cites George Ticknor's goals for the Boston Public Library as an example of Ticknor's motivation for the library to serve an educational purpose:

> (1) To educate the masses so that they would follow the "best men" and not demagogues; to "stabilize the Republic and to keep America from becoming another Carthage."
> (2) To provide access to the world's best books for that elite minority who would someday become leaders of the political, intellectual, and moral affairs of the nation.[7]

While education remains the top priority, it is given a different direction and motivation. Ticknor was not educating people so they could fully explore their potential and make decisions on their own; he was advocating education to maintain social and political control over the masses.

The rise of the immigrant worker and the potential destabilizing effect this could have on the society was well known to the politicians and library leaders of the time. Between 1880 and 1900, over 9,000,000 people immigrated to the United States, followed by an additional 14,000,000 between 1901 and 1920. These were huge numbers of people to assimilate and make into Americans. Because of this, libraries became not only places of education, but education with a purpose, to educate and mainstream the growing immigrant class and the large urban populations of the eastern cities.

So while education remained a goal, it was a goal with a different purpose, and that difference of purpose reflects a basic conflict that is ongoing in libraries. If, as Ticknor states, the goal of education was to make the "best men," someone had to take on the responsibility for determining what were the qualities and characteristics of the "best men." The library would then determine what path it should take to achieve that goal. The library's assumption of the moral responsibility for creating the "best men" through education and the use of the library would be a continuing force throughout library history, surfacing now and again with questions regarding fiction, collection development, and intellectual freedom controversies.

For those familiar with library history, the emergence of groups such as Family Friendly Libraries, who are attempting to bring library policies across the country into alignment with their moral ideals, can be seen merely as a return to the role of the library as moral arbiter. Fixing the role of the library as truly that of moral arbiter places it in direct conflict with the values of neutrality and intellectual freedom that developed about half a century ago and have become central to our shared vision of libraries.

How can the profession reconcile these two conflicting concepts? For many contemporary librarians the easiest way has been to say that the moral agenda of the first librarians has long been abandoned by the profession. The profession has moved into the era of neutrality and intellectual freedom. While this is an easy answer, it may not be entirely true. The conflict over what type of educational institution the library should be is still raised in issues such as collection development, access and technology.

The view of the library as the uplifter of the common person may be an even more accepted part of both library and American folk history. Libraries have been portrayed as the refuge of the ordinary man, publicly supported to ensure that lack of money was no barrier to the acquisition of knowledge. In 1884, Moses Coit Taylor addressed the opening of the West Bay City, Michigan, library with the following observation about the founding of the first subscription library by Benjamin Franklin in 1731.

> But in 1731, by that modest device of Benjamin Franklin, the democratic spirit—the modern humane spirit—the spirit which in its true nature is a leveling spirit only in this grand sense that it levels upward and not downward, and raises the general average of human intelligence and felicity—this benign and mighty democratic spirit, I say, which was then marching with gentle but invincible footsteps along all avenues and pathways of modern life, and was laying its miraculous touch on church and state, on kings and priests and peasants, on the laws and lawmakers, on all the old activities of society, on the old adjustments of human relations, that spirit then began to touch this relation also, the relation of man to the superb and royal realm of books. And the first effect of that touch was what? it was enlargement, liberalization, extension of intellectual opportunity for man simply as man. Hitherto books had been the privilege of the privileged class. In effect, Franklin says: they shall be so no more.[8]

This view of libraries as the great democratizing force is one that is consistently published to the public and presented in library literature. George Ticknor, in addition to establishing the "best man" theory for the Boston Public Library, also held firm beliefs regarding the library's role in social change.

He asserted that man was perfectible and that books were the principle means of obtaining that perfection.[9] These beliefs in the ability of books to increase man's perfection and the library as the place which enabled that development have been common themes in the stated purposes of American libraries. A library was viewed as a place to which worker and employer would have equal access; the conventions of class and income would have no sway. The poor may be poor but at least in the library there would be the opportunity for equality.

The role of the library as the great democratizing force is, however, one that has been problematic, and as we will see, there are persuasive alternatives to this view. But for good or ill, it remains that for many the library is seen as a place of democracy, disseminating materials that will give the ordinary citizen the knowledge needed to become an informed member of society. It is the refuge of the displaced and the poor, another concept being challenged by questions regarding the use of libraries by the homeless and the provision of service for fees.

The role of the library as the great democratizer is also challenged by recent library history revisionists. As Dee Garrison states, in analyzing the content and speeches at the 1876 public librarian convention it became clear that for the participants, "Although the primary purpose (of the library) was clearly educational, the function of the library as a social stabilizer—a motive that had played so large a part in British library development—was also present in American minds."[10]

The role of the great democratizer is then placed in contrast with the role of a social stabilizer. The two were perhaps synonymous for many. If the population embraced American democracy and the values that it encompassed, then the society would be a stable one without the conflict that seemed imminent with the rise of labor unions, alternative political parties and the increasing urbanization of the United States. For some, however, the interpretation of the role of the library as the great democratizer led in a different direction; it led to the library's being a place of divergent ideals that the citizen could use either to overthrow the current system or to embrace it. The story of Karl Marx studying in the British Library and then writing *Das Kapital* would strike terror in some. In others it would be a wonderful example of the true spirit of human inquiry that the library could and should nurture.

It was also clear that in reality the library was not a refuge for the poor or a place where the worker and boss would sit side by side. All data indicate that from the very beginning public libraries have been institutions bred of middle class values which cater to that group. Dee Garrison cites a 1895 library survey which showed that only 20 percent of the population used the public library; almost all of them were professionals, women and children.[11]

While lip service may have been given to the welcoming concept of a place open to all, the reality was that libraries were cold, forbidding places where patrons were expected to wash their hands before getting books and where lessons in manners were as freely given as the books themselves.

In addition to the view of the library as educator and the great democratizer, many librarians saw the role of the library as an instrument of culture. The library is the place where true civilization will take place in society. In 1904 Hugo Munsterberg, professor of psychology at Harvard, said in his book *The Americans*, "Thus the public library has come to be a recognized instrument of culture along with the public school; and in all American outposts the school teacher and librarians are among the pioneers."[12] So the expectation has now become that the library is a force for culture and civilization along with a force for education and democracy. This statement assumes that there is a consensus about what the culture is and what it should be. However true this might have been in 1904, as the twentieth century progressed and America become more culturally diverse, the assumption that there is an accepted cultural norm and the inherent problems that arise from that assumption became a key issue in contemporary librarianship.

The view of libraries as cultural centers was interpreted more broadly in early libraries than may be common today. "Cultural center" also included the concept of the library as social and community center, a vital component in the life of the community. Margery Quigley, librarian of the Divoll Branch of the St. Louis Public Library, writes in a special report on social work that libraries were meeting places for clubs and that branches would have up to 52 club meetings a year. Not just meetings, but birthday parties, dances, and social activities were the norms of the day at many libraries. And while she did not advocate librarians' becoming social workers, she did suggest that the need might exist for a social worker to be part of the library staff. While she stated that for many the uses of the library included the pursuit of knowledge and books, she was clearly not upset with others who used the library solely as a cultural and social center.[13]

David William Davies, writing in *Libraries as Cultural and Social Centers*, documents how libraries in England and the United States responded to this vision of the library as the cultural center of the community. Common activities included the performing arts, arts and crafts exhibits, public readings, art exhibitions. In some cases the library actually merged with the municipal museum or concert hall.[14]

The public library of today may still claim culture as part of its purpose and many libraries still engage in activities similar to those described by Davies, but the vision of the library as social service agency is no longer the norm. Such a social service concept did resurface at times throughout the history of American public libraries, usually to fade in the face of changing political values. The public library responded to the Depression and to the social activism of the 1960s and 1970s with social services, but these programs fell away in time. Today social outreach programs such as literacy and community services are seldom considered core activities and are often funded through grants and other similar sources.

All three of these potentially problematic purposes for the library will come into play as we begin to examine some specific and universal concerns in library service: collection development, access issues, reference services, intellectual freedom and the concept of the neutrality of information.

Collection Development: From the "Fiction Problem" to the "Internet Problem"

A recurrent theme in library history from 1900 to the present is the problem of collection development. What should a library collect, what guidelines should be used, who should be the arbiter of what to collect, what is the role of the individual patron in determining collection development policies, and what is the role of the community? These questions, perhaps phrased differently, or in different contexts, have challenged librarians, and in particular public librarians, for a long time.

For many early librarians these questions were easily answered because of the firm belief in the mission and purpose of the library. If the purpose of the library was to educate, to uplift and, depending upon one's interpretation of library history, to socialize the masses into proper citizens, then the materials to be purchased should be the classics. The character of a person could be determined by the books he or she read—which should be of such quality and value that there would be no doubt that it would uplift and inform. Whether to purchase popular fiction was not an issue since education and moral uplift were the ultimate purpose of the library.

The fiction question, however, was not that easily solved. For many patrons the impetus to come to the library was to have access to the newest fiction. The growing publishing industry of the late 1800s was creating best sellers and contemporary literature at a startling pace and the average citizen hoped and expected to find those materials at the library. The librarian's dilemma over acquiring popular fiction was of no small matter; limited resources, the need for accountability to governing boards, and the honor of a new and burgeoning profession made the decisions very difficult.

Various rationales were put forward to allay fears that the library would merely be pandering to popular taste if fiction were included in the collection. One rationale was that the role of the library as an educator was crucial and therefore fiction could be incorporated into the educational mission of the library if it assisted the library in meeting the education goal.

This theory (called the "taste-elevation theory" by Williams in the chapter entitled "The Fiction Problem" in *The American Public Library and the*

Problem of Purpose, supposed that patrons, and in particular children, needed to develop a taste for reading. It became the library's job to introduce them to popular fiction and then develop their taste as they grew so that by the time they reached adulthood they would have put away novels and embraced the more classical literature of the refined mind.[15] This same rationale was used with nonreading adults and the immigrant populations. These groups were not expected to be at the same intellectual level as others, and in order to enjoy reading they would need to begin at a much lower reading level.

The popular fiction question was also viewed from the aspect of the moral role of the library. While it was a given that popular fiction was not on the same literary level with the classics, distinctions were made between popular fiction that promoted the moral uplift that was the library mission, and fiction that produced moral and social decay. Librarians felt justified in acquiring, if not promoting, some "good" fiction and excluding those works which would lead to the decline of civilization.

Dee Garrison states that a common belief about fiction was that "the inveterate novel reader often acquired a craving for constant excitement. So stimulated, a reader lost his sober judgment and resigned himself to life's afflictions. Fictional characters and scenes that gave false conceptions of duty, honor, and life would unsettle the morals of even the most virtuous reader."[16] If books had such power, then it was imperative for the librarian to determine which books would lead the reader down the path to moral decay and expunge those books from the library.

The idea of the librarian's acting as a moral agent in the selection of materials would not be tolerated in most libraries today. But librarians still do make decisions regarding what to purchase, and from an ever increasing amount of literature. At the turn of the century the expansion of the publishing industry gave librarians justification for making selections based on morals. The number of books being published was too great even then for the public library to buy them all. Today the number of books published has only increased and librarians are as always forced to make judgments regarding what to purchase.

The creation of collection development policies allows the library to outline the major areas in which it will acquire material and how the selection and acquisition should be carried out. However, distinctions between good and bad books are still made in response to the mission of the library. Debates still rage around fiction, how much to purchase, how many copies to purchase, whether the library should purchase only materials that meet popular demand, or purchase the works of "literature" that will stand the test of time.

In 1990, a classics reprint series in *Library Journal* presented two articles and an editorial from past issues dealing with the problems of collection development. One article was from 1897 by W.M. Stevenson and the second was by Nora Rawlinson published in 1981; the editorial, from 1979, was by *Library*

Journal editor John Berry. These three essays reflect the continuing debate surrounding popular literature.

Stevenson's assertion is that while some books, such as those by Horatio Alger and Mrs. E.D.E.N. Southworth, may not be immoral, they are not literature and do not deserve a place on the library shelves. He says that the theory that reading fiction will improve the public's taste in literature is utterly false. Stevenson chastised librarians who continue to justify fiction purchases on the basis of its leading the reader to a better quality of literature. The fact that libraries report increases in fiction circulation proves to him that this theory does not work. He states that the only rationale for the library to exist is as an educational institution, and that if it is purely a form of entertainment, it has no right to expect public support.[17]

This view was not shared by all librarians at the time and would find little support now, but similar sentiments were expressed in a 1990 editorial by John Berry in musing upon the Baltimore County book selection policy described in Nora Rawlinson's above cited 1981 *Library Journal* article. Berry supports the necessity of "quality" book selection and bemoans selection based solely on public demand.[18] This view of librarians as keepers of culture and not as institutions to be built around public caprice would have found favor with Stevenson in 1897.

Rawlinson, then book selector for Baltimore County Public Library, writes that the job of the library is to respond to the needs of the public. Book circulation is the best indicator of whether a book should be retained, she contends, and therefore use and requests become the driving determinants of purchase decisions. She makes it clear that the public does not want solely fiction and that if the classics and nonfiction are available they are there because of demand and not because of the library's wish to be a cultural warehouse of knowledge.[19]

So while the battlefield may no longer be over whether we should have fiction, it may have moved to how much fiction we should have and what is the role of nonfiction and the classics in today's customer driven market. These questions raise ethical concerns about the role of the library in response to its clientele and what the true role of the librarian is in collection development.

In the current information age these same questions are raised in a technological guise. Should libraries allow access to the potential moral threat of the Internet and the World Wide Web? Is this the contemporary equivalent of the fiction problem of the early 20th century? Like the librarians of a hundred years ago, some respond by not allowing these problematic resources in the door: If they do not offer it, there is no problem. Some, like their long ago counterparts, decide to offer only the best of the Internet. Decisions are made about providing access to a careful, thoughtful selection of material that would meet the public's need but still maintain a high level of value.

Some libraries may choose screening programs, others block individual URL's in an effort to provide only the "best" to their patrons. Unfortunately, the attempt to provide only the "best," while it may have worked with books, is not a workable option. The very nature of the Internet means that such an approach, no matter how rational and defensible, cannot succeed unless the technology itself changes. The growth of new sites and the rigidness of screening programs makes today's solutions inadequate to deal with the future.

When we consider the fiction problem of the late 1800s, it is easy to see it as much ado about nothing. The books that were considered questionable would probably be considered mainstream, if not prudish, in the light of current fiction available in libraries. It is also possible that with changing tastes and values, the contemporary concerns over the Internet will also be viewed as narrow and moralistic. But we must remember that librarians operate in a specific social and moral environment and within a specific community. Librarians cannot take themselves completely out of that environment when making decisions regarding collection development. Librarians may choose to ignore certain aspects of the culture or the community to provide a service that they feel is important but that decision is still judged by the values of the time and the place in which it is made.

For any ethical or moral stance to be taken, there needs to be an acknowledgment that certain values and standards can be identified and followed. In the contemporary world of librarianship many deny that collection development decisions will have moral implications. Many librarians hold the reassuring belief that all information is neutral and therefore the library's collection development decisions do not involve judgments about whether some information is good or bad. But for many librarians and community activists this is not the case. The belief that some information is morally wrong and that the use of these resources can lead to moral decay reflects the same concern of early library leaders.

If there are similarities between the fiction problem and the current concern for what types of online access to provide, does the outcome of the fiction problem provide us a solution to the online problem?

Apparently the solution for the fiction problem was time—actually about a quarter century. This was enough time for the public's persistent demand for fiction to wear down the library establishment, time for librarians to admit that fiction and recreational reading may have a place in the library, and time for librarians to give up their vision of the library as a solely educational and cultural center.

Will time have the same effect on the Internet question? The passage of time will certainly allow the library to accurately gauge the public's true interest in the Internet and it will allow the pioneering libraries, who are forging ahead with Internet access, time to develop policies and procedures that the rest of the library world can follow. Time will also allow the public library in particular to think through its new and evolving mission in the "information age," and it will allow the technology to further develop so that a technological fix for the problems presented might be realistic.

It is also important to note that while the fiction problem for the majority of American public librarians ended around 1900, undercurrents of concern and ongoing questions regarding the suitability of some fiction are still present. Ester Jane Carrier documented fifty years of continuing struggle in her book *Fiction in Public Libraries, 1900–1950*.[20] The Public Library Inquiry of 1947 suggested that libraries cut back on their fiction. Struggles persist over censorship, the immorality of certain literature and the library's role in limiting access to certain morally questionable fiction. So if our parallel between the two problems is still valid, it is safe to say that neither problem will ever truly be resolved. Old visions of the past become endowed with the nostalgia of a lost time, and for some the golden age of librarianship might become the time when books were the sole rulers and the Internet was a vision of writers of science fiction.

Collection development of Internet materials is also problematic since it makes librarians approach selection in a different way. Libraries and librarians have developed elaborate collection development policies and analyzed how to spend limited resources on the most appropriate materials for their collections. While libraries may differ on what to buy, for the most part selection decisions are made in a rational and logical manner. The Internet, on the other hand, changes the library's task from selection to deselection.

The Internet is a force with no discriminations of quality, and none of the filtering mechanisms that librarians have traditionally relied on to assist in making collection development decisions. Our traditional selections come from the highly filtered mainstream publishing industry with some small and alternative press materials also available. While this is a large body of material, it contains information that has been heavily screened and presented to the public and libraries as acceptable.

Such filtering does not take place on the Internet, so the library is presented with material that may fall outside of that range of acceptability. This means that librarians must make all decisions regarding the appropriateness, accuracy, and value of material on the Internet if we approach it in the same way we approach book selection. Since this is an impractical task given the volume of Internet resources, libraries must develop new ways of thinking to justify their Internet access policy.

While there are parallels between the two historical problems, what is dramatically different is the present-day library's fear of litigation. In the days of concerns about the fiction problem, clergy and teachers were all willing to offer opinions about what libraries should collect, but there was little thought that the library would be sued or held legally responsible for the contents of its collection. The legal atmosphere of the technological age may be taking away from libraries the time to adjust, make mistakes, and define and refine their role in the provision of information technology.

The Internet problem has many different solutions depending upon which mission of the library is emphasized. When education is considered the primary focus of the library, the need for Internet access for all becomes a primary concern. The amount of information that is available can aid and assist patrons of all ages and educational levels in expanding their knowledge base and giving them new insights into how people think and feel. While the recreational aspects of the Internet may have less educational value, the line between educational and recreation becomes blurred on many of the Internet sites. So, while some aspects may not meet the educational goal, it may be hard to exclude them. Providing Internet access also provides individuals without the resources to buy computers access to information that would not be available to them otherwise just as the library provides books to those who could not afford them.

The role of the library as moral arbiter makes Internet access much more problematic for many librarians and patrons. If the role of the library is to provide only materials that will assist the patron with their moral development, the amount of suspect material available on the Internet makes it a questionable place for adults and a scary place for children. But as we have seen with the fiction problem most libraries have moved away from the role of moral arbiter. The reasons are, variously, an inability to define what moral values the library should uphold, the public's demand for literature and services that are more recreational in nature, and a societal shift in direction toward intellectual freedom and access to all information by all patrons. This diminishing of the moral role of the library does not mean that the moral aspects of the Internet will not be problematic, but if that role no longer holds for print materials it cannot be held as the standard for nonprint materials.

The role of cultural center would seem to favor the use of the Internet; the wide range of sites that are available can expand and enhance a library's collection and make it more valuable to the members of the community. Internet access will draw people into the library and be a basis for programming, educational, and cultural activities.

As we can see, using historical reflection to help define the library's purpose will also help the library define what their response should be to the provision of Internet access just as their definition of purpose currently drives book purchases. Collection development policies are reflections of the library's effort first to identify and then to support its mission and role in the community; electronic resources are just an additional component of that plan.

Accessibility Issues

In conjunction with collection development decisions and problems, the library at the turn of the century looked for ways to get around the potentially damaging effects of some of their materials. Solutions that were devised included the development of separate collections for distinct patron groups, and the limitation on access to materials. These solutions protected the reader from inappropriate books and protected the books from potential abuse or theft by the reader.

The public library moved more quickly than academic libraries to open the stacks to the public, but not without discussion and controversy. The following passage from Ditzion (1947) summarizes the major concerns of that era regarding open shelves.

> Access to bookstacks, though at first conceived as a privilege of highest desireability for student and scholarly readers, was later argued on the basis of serving the workingman's need. The "closed shelfers" maintained that an intelligent desk attendant would be more helpful to the "lower class men" than admission to the stacks. ... Of course, the closed-shelf school thought that open access would be abused by the less educated common folk and would result not only in the disorder of the libraries's shelves but also in the loss of books by outright theft.[21]

In this passage the conflicting roles of preservation and use are expressed. This duality has raised a variety of ethical questions. Why do libraries exist? and What type of access should be provided.

All types of libraries have acknowledged their role as preservers of knowledge. Some feel academic libraries have a greater interest in preservation, but public libraries also strive to preserve and protect the materials that have been purchased for public use. Ironically, it is often impossible to protect materials from the public for whom one has purchased them! Libraries that are mere storehouses of information hold little interest for the public. The more attractive library resources are to the public, the more likely they will be damaged through negligent use or overuse.

Ditzion touches on some of the main issues of the open/closed stacks argument. Some have defended closed stacks mainly out of the fear of loss and misplacement of materials. Also of concern was the provision of the best service to the patron, and the potential of placing the library patron in moral danger of becoming a thief.

Seventy years ago Isabel Ely Lord presented another aspect of the issue: "The question, then, to be decided is whether the privilege of open shelves is a demoralizing influence in a community because it suggests or encourages theft? Does it, in other words, make thieves?"[22]

The idea that the patron must be protected from the potentially corrupting effect of open shelves is also reflected in the use of restricted collections.

Librarians were worried not only that users might become thieves but that they might also be in danger of coming in contact with corrupting moral values. The development of restricted collections ensured that the general public was not allowed to see material that was sensitive or immoral in nature, since that might increase the patron's proclivity for improper behavior.

The idea that open shelves were not providing the best service was reflected in the argument that the patron needed reference assistance. To set the patrons free to roam the shelves without trained help was an abandonment of the patron and not to be recommended. Willcox states that "...the advocates of the open shelf forget this, the most important function of the library—the duty of helping the helpless.... These readers can all without exception be more promptly and satisfactorily served through the printed fiction list and bulletins by the assistants at the desk."[23] Thus Willcox proposes that better service is provided by closed stacks. He assumes that the patron is "helpless" and in need of guidance by the superior intellectual skills and moral fiber of the librarian.

In spite of the moral arguments presented by Willcox and others closed stacks were largely a phenomena of the past at most public libraries by the early 1900s. The fear of moral decline and the loss of material could not withstand the public's enthusiastic response to open shelves and the increased access that they provided. Improving classification and access tools along with printed bibliographies and finding aids also assisted the patron in becoming a more independent user of the library, free to roam the open shelves.

Academic libraries also underwent a period of profound change from 1875 to 1900. Collections were increasing rapidly, and access to collections was also a growing concern. Prior to this time, many academic collections were housed in closed stacks with very restricted hours, and at some universities undergraduates had no borrowing privileges at all. The change in the type of research that academic institutions were undertaking and the increasing collection sizes also led to new attitudes regarding access. Harvard went from 48 hours of service per week in 1876 to 82 hours in 1986, Yale increased from 36 to 72 hours in the same period, and Columbia, under the leadership of Melvil Dewey, went from 12 hours a week in 1876 to 102 hours in 1888.[24]

Increased hours combined with some changes in access to the stacks and reference collections in the academic setting paralleled the dramatic changes taking place in public libraries. The Columbia University library, in addition to expanding its hours, also opened its stacks to students and faculty. A reference librarian at Columbia wrote in 1891 that "the popularity of the library was largely due to the unrestricted access to the shelves."[25] (It also appears that the fear of theft was of less concern to Columbia than to public libraries because of the university's "higher class of readers"![26])

Access to library materials for children was not a normal component of libraries at the beginning of the public library movement. A minimum age for acquiring a library card was a common feature of public libraries; in some libraries the minimum age was as high as 18. The beginnings of library service to children may have started with the Pawtucket, Rhode Island, public library that in 1877 was the first to allow children under the age of 12 to use books.[27] The opening of collections to children again raised the fiction question: Should children be exposed to the potential evils of immoral fiction?

Regarding children's literature, it appears that the question was more easily resolved; fiction was approved only through the aggressive censorship of materials. No effort was spared to ensure that only quality books would be available. The advent of separate children's areas, with the librarian there to regulate materials and offer guidance, assured the child's moral safety and the development of good taste in reading materials. This type of controlled environment, which did not allow access to adult materials, was prevalent in public libraries well into the 1960s and 1970s.

In the professional arena it was very much the same. Protection from discrimination in access based on age was first added to the Library Bill of Rights in 1967, and the Library Bill of Rights Interpretation on Free Access to Minors was first approved in 1972. These professional statements on the right of minors to access all library materials acknowledged the shift in the role of the library from protecting the young from potentially harmful materials to giving that responsibility to the children and their parents. While the policy of denying children access to the entire book collection is no longer practiced, it becomes a consideration when librarians face the potential problem of Internet access. Librarians and parents may be comfortable giving the child access to all adult book materials but may wonder if Internet access may lead to the moral corruption that was so feared a hundred years ago.

What is the difference then between libraries' clear statements on rights of children to access the library and the concerns regarding the access of children to the Internet? For many it might be the format of the material. Librarians have learned how to deal with words but do not know how to effectively deal with pictures. When discussions take place about the abuse of the Internet, it is not normally the text that raises concerns; it is the graphics. Somehow we have been able to justify and defend words that depict and even promote sexual or offensive acts but when presented with a graphic representation of the same act we do not know how to defend it—or more to the point, we do not know whether we should defend it.

Our defense of words has many debatable aspects to it but one thing it does do is separate the literate from the illiterate. To a child without the vocabulary or interest in literature, adult works with explicit accounts of sex or violence hold little attraction. Pictures, however, even if their context is not totally understood, can raise questions and be considered inappropriate for preliterate and minimally literate audiences.

Librarians have dealt previously with the graphics issue but mainly in the areas of the relatively new graphic novel, some art books and perpetual discussions of *Playboy*. Collection development plays a key role in this area also. We feel that in the traditional library we are able to select material that meets the established criteria of our collection development policy, and we can safely exclude material that meets the legal definition of pornography. With the openness of the Internet, this distinction becomes much more problematic.

The question of access is obviously more complex than just the question of whether to have open or closed stacks or to allow children access to the entire collection. Access issues also include the catalog and cataloging practices, equal access to all library services regardless of ability to pay, and accessibility to the collection for the physically challenged. In these areas the growth of technology has brought new problems and new potential solutions to the question of access.

The contemporary online catalog, with links to a larger bibliographic utility, allows access to a quantity of materials that is exponentially greater than a single library's holdings. The increased level of access brings the problem of availability. In a world increasingly driven by fees, does an individual's ability to pay affect the availability of information to him or her? These fees may include cost recovery for interlibrary loan, holds, transfers, etc. In the case of fee-based services such as online searching the ability to pay may remove access to the service itself.

A hundred years ago, when the stacks were closed, exceptions were often made to allow "worthy" patrons into the stacks so they could browse. In most cases the definition of worthy equaled, if not wealth, a social standing that would equate with acceptable behavior. In the library's embrace of fees for service, are we again using the same criteria to limit access, not to the shelves this time but to the online databases and other fee-based services?

Unlike the patrons who knew they were being denied access to the open shelves and who requested that this change, the patron denied access to an online database because of inability to pay may be only dimly aware of the potential of the resource since it is not a tangible object such as a book. These patrons may be more resigned to the loss, but the loss of information that could be helpful to them is still a problem, especially if the new resources, for which fees are required, are purchased with funds formerly use for other more traditional media.

The question of access by those with physical or mental impairments is a different kind of access question. While the shelves and services are open to them, does the format provided truly meet their information needs? For many years the library community met this challenge by the establishment of such services as state libraries for the blind. With increasingly effective technology it is now possible for libraries to have such equipment as Kurzweil readers, computer programs which enlarge text and other devices that would allow patrons access to the local collection. Does the local library have an obligation to provide that type of access?

The question may again be who pays—the same question that was raised when open access to the shelves was at issue. Librarians had not only moral issues but also monetary ones. If the books were stolen, who was going to pay to replace them? Does the same concern govern our decisions to provide complete access to our collections?

Access issues again call into question the mission of the library. If librarians are educators because they believe it is desirable for patrons to discover new sources of information and to make the kind of serendipitous finds that occur only when given free rein to roam the library, then the educational mission would lead us to support the concept of free and equal access to all. But if our definition of the educational mission involves the proactive attention and concern of a trained professional then it might be argued that such otherwise antiquated notions as closed access provided better service because they require the attention of a library worker who could assist in the location of materials and provide the added value that is not a part of a self-service library.

While this latter view was espoused during the open/closed stack debates, it does not promote the type of education that the library does best: the spontaneous search for information and the ability to look at books and materials without the intervention of an authority figure who might question or impinge upon the individual. So the educational mission that emerges is one that values the individual's right to locate and use information but also provides, as we shall see in the next section, skilled personnel to give the guidance and knowledge needed by the individual to best use the resources available both in the library and elsewhere.

The question of "moral uplift" was also an element in making access decisions: the opening of stacks, the eventual elimination of "reserved" sections for questionable materials, and the end of restricted access for children. The cumulative effect of these decisions is that the library withdrew as the moral arbiter of the community. The library was giving the individual the right and responsibility for making decisions regarding what they read and what books best met their needs regardless of the potential moral outcomes of such reading.

Opening and expanding access to the library also increased the library's value as a community center and perhaps as a cultural center. The decision to open the stacks was a reflection of the library community trust and willingness to turn the entire library over to the public. This type of trust was one of the necessary steps in presenting the library as the heart of the community and a place open for discussion and the pursuit of knowledge.

These access questions are interesting and complex, and the answers to them are just as multidimensional. The solutions reflect the profession's ongoing refinement and adjustment of its mission and role in the life of society. Looking back at this history may allow us to see the issues more clearly.

Reference Services

Historically speaking, reference service began much later than the collection development issues we have been discussing. Academic libraries had been in existence in America since the 1700s, but until the late 1800s they were basically warehouses of material with a custodian who had the title of librarian and whose main job was to collect and organize the materials and keep them from being used, lost, or stolen. The public librarian from the 1850s on was busy establishing libraries, building collections, processing materials and worrying about the fiction problem, access to the collection, and other issues. However, as the end of the century approached, libraries started to believe that reference service to individuals was important and that librarians could and should do more than just provide access to the materials that they collected.

One of the first proposals for reference service was presented by Samuel Swett Green of the Worcester Free Public Library at the 1876 conference of librarians. Green's paper, "The Desireableness of Establishing Personal Intercourse and Relations Between Librarians and Readers in Popular Libraries," presented the proposal that the ordinary patrons were often unable to easily find the books that they required and that it was the job of the library to offer such assistance as was necessary to help these patrons locate materials.[28] While Green's proposal may seem to be a modest one, it was one of the first acknowledgments that the library might have any role at all in the provision of personal service to the patron.

Green proposed that the library help guide the reader to appropriate books as well as provide information requested by the patron. He presented a case for the hiring of educated, intelligent, and friendly people who would be available to library users in need of assistance. While he agreed that the library catalog had benefited the reader, he felt that the user must be trained to use it effectively, and that training and instruction was also the role of the librarian.

Green's proposal was met with varying levels of acceptance throughout the country, and while public libraries were then beginning to look upon some level of personal assistance as a worthwhile service, the academic community also had in Melvil Dewey at Columbia their model of reference service. Dewey's vision of library service, much like Green's, included the provision of reference service and made the assumption that with the increasing number of library materials available, the library user would have to rely on a trained and intelligent reference librarian for assistance in using the collection efficiently and effectively.

The addition of a reference department to the Columbia library and the appointment of two reference librarians to that department as early as 1884 was a model for other institutions to follow.[29] But Dewey's model was to remain the exception rather than the rule at most universities for a number of years. Harvard, for example, did not have a formal Reference Department until 1915, and this was true for many other university and college libraries.

The public libraries were quicker to follow Green's lead, and for many the provision of catalog assistance and other forms of public service such as reference and referral became an integral part of library service. As the service developed, so did questions regarding what was appropriate reference service for librarians to offer and what should be provided to the public. For most public libraries, reference service still focused on aiding the patron in using the card catalog and locating materials. This would gradually change over the course of the twentieth century to include the more factual reference questions that are handled today in public libraries.

The discussion of ethics in the reference setting does not, however, seem to have been a major concern or even of much interest to the profession. Wendell Johnson points out that "ethics" is not, as it were, a topic in discussions of reference services to be found in library literature, and even professional articles about ethics in general infrequently focus on reference services.[30]

Michael McCoy, in his article "Bibliographic Overview: The Ethics of Reference Service," traces the history of ethical discussions regarding the provision of reference service and finds that most discussions of the topic focus on the attempt to reconcile the ideal of reference service with actual practice.[31] Historically, the library literature has focused on what level of service to provide, how much time to spend with patrons, and what depth of answer to provide, but very little discourse occurs on what types of questions may be inappropriate or even unethical for the librarian to answer.

With the development of the Library Bill of Rights and other intellectual freedom statements, the issue of reference ethics became synonymous with the intellectual freedom issue, and the professional stance was that no judgment could be applied to the information request and that all requests would be answered as fully and objectively as possible.

The issue of ethical neutrality was the main concern of Robert Hauptman's classic experiment asking reference librarians for information on how to build a bomb. Hauptman puts forward the argument that the abandonment of an ethical commitment to the patron because of a professional responsibility to oppose censorship denies the individual librarian's personal responsibility to the greater good of the patron and society.[32] For many, this argument articulated one of the main ethical concerns in reference work.

While Hauptman considers the provision of value-neutral reference service problematic, John Swan, in a dialogue with Hauptman published in *Catholic Library World,* argues that as persons and librarians we have no way to accurately judge intent, and to make assumptions about intent from a patron's question is overstepping the bounds of the profession.[33] This distinction between the intent and the request itself is one way of handling the moral problem presented in Hauptman's experiment.

These types of ethical dilemmas seem to appear only in the library literature of the later twentieth century. It is also true that Samuel Green's 1876 article, which first proposed the institution of reference service, also provided some guidelines for appropriate response to questions that may be controversial. Green states that the librarian should "avoid scrupulously the propagation of any particular set of views in politics, art, history, philosophy or theology"[34]—a statement very much in keeping with modern-day views of intellectual freedom. (Unfortunately, Green does not offer an opinion on whether to answer ethically questionable inquires. One wonders if it even occurred to him that librarians would be put in a position to answer such questions.)

If the issue of how to handle ethically questionable inquiries is placed in the context of the historical missions of the library—educator, moral arbiter, cultural center—it is possible to see how conflicting thoughts on the topic would arise. If the library is a place of education, then answers to such questions should emphasize assisting the patron in developing a well thought out inquiry and teaching the skills necessary to answer the question. The role of the library as moral arbiter might bring a different perspective.

If the question is one that will encourage the individual to engage in morally repugnant behavior, then the question is one that should not be answered. If books were chosen on the basis of their moral nature, and collections were closed in order to prevent the library from encouraging theft, then what rationale could the librarian of the late 1800s use to assist a patron in building a bomb or engaging in unlawful activities? In Hauptman's informal survey and the more formal experiment conducted by Dowd regarding freebasing cocaine,[35] some librarians supplied the answer but showed some moral concerns about supplying the information. The use of the library for promoting immoral activity is a hard concept to justify. Perhaps that is why libraries still insist that they are buying *Playboy*, and patrons say they are borrowing the magazine, for the quality of the articles.

This moral dilemma, like most library ethics problems, takes on an added dimension with the advent of increased computerization and new technology. When the librarian controlled reference resources through purchase or exclusive use, collection development policies and personal ethics could be used to determine what type of question to answer and what kind of material should be provided to the public. With the increased access to databases and the

Internet, the patron may be able to find information that even the reference librarian would not consider it their duty to supply. Does the library have any responsibility to protect the patron and society from the one who would use library resources, if not library personnel, for purposes that are morally reprehensible? Does the neutrality of information carry over to all the information that can be available on the Internet?

The move from an educational and moral model to a more recreational and public driven institution is reflected in another aspect of reference, the provision of service. How much information should a patron be provided with, and how should the allocation of reference services be determined in a potentially scarce resource environment?

For years the education model of the library influenced the depth of information provided. The library was an educational institution, and the responsibility of the librarian was to show the patron how to use the various reference tools, or, more generally, to provide patrons with the skills necessary to find the information they needed. This type of educational model is still strong in the academic and school environment but as the educational mission of the public library changed so did the expectations of the public regarding what level of reference service should be provided.

Rothstein, in his history of reference service, sees a gradual shift during the early twentieth century from the "conservative theory" of reference, card catalog assistance, and minimal direct answers, to the more proactive "moderate" approach, which would include what we now consider to be ready reference, telephone reference, and the provision of direct information.[36] This move is in keeping with the shift from the educational library to the recreational and patron demand driven library that has changed our approach to collection development and access.

Members of the public look to the library to provide them not only with an educational experience but with a customer-driven, on-demand service which supplies answers and does not necessarily provide an educational function. While the reality appears to be a shift away from the educational model, many reference librarians in the public library sector, when asked, would still define their role as educational, in deference to the historical mission and thrust of the public library.

Another factor in patron service has been the level of staffing. The level of patron service in most libraries has been dictated by the number of library employees who are available, and while it is an accepted ethical stance that all patrons should receive as much help as they need, it is a reality that staffing shortages and increased patron demands mean that libraries and librarians do not have the time to meet the patrons' needs as fully as they would like. As Rothstein notes, conscientious librarians may often feel that they are short changing the patron if they follow the library's policy of limiting service in the interest of economy.[37]

There have been few models proposed for how to deal with the problem of service inequity at the reference desk. Wendell Johnson believes in the need for a value-based policy and uses the philosophy of John Rawls to set up library equivalents of "principles of justice" which govern how reference service should be allocated among various kinds of patron demands. The value-based approach was first developed by G.E. Koster and states that the value of justice can be applied to library reference policies. That application of justice then leads to a value based approach to reference service.[38]

Johnson, using the value-based approach, develops a model which provides an ethical framework for allocating resources; it is one of the few examples of trying to place reference ethics within a larger philosophical context.[39] But in reality, most questions of service end up being determined by budget and organizational missions and goals, with the front line reference librarians being put in the ethical wasteland of not being able to provide the level of service they may feel is their ethical and moral obligation to their patrons. With the advent of new technology this problem becomes even more acute.

New types of services such as the Internet, online searching, and CD-ROM products give librarians more responsibility to impart a wider range of information to patrons. They also have the additional duties of maintaining equipment, putting paper in printers, and keeping the new technological infrastructure up and running. These increased demands place the reference librarian in an even more time constricted and limiting position in regard to truly satisfying the patron's needs.

In examining the various missions of the library in regard to reference services, it is again easy to see the conflicts that arise between the educational mission and the moral uplift vision of the library. If the library is truly educational, then issues regarding what type of reference service to provide and what questions to answer would be moot. The individual's request and need for information would take precedence over the potential moral harm that would arise out of reference inquiry. Much of the concern expressed by Hauptman and others can be directly related to the view of the library as a place of moral uplift and preserver of virtue. The relinquishment of this role in the reference setting has for the most part been accomplished, but the underlying uneasiness of totally abandoning that role can be seen in articles questioning the provision of all type of reference service and the failure of the library community to find common ethical codes or guidelines for the provision of reference service.

The role of the library as cultural center has diminished with the increased emphasis on reference services in most libraries. With fewer resources, the programs and services that place the library as a key player in the cultural community have often been sacrificed to provide a minimal level of reference service. The library has become a provider of specific information needs to a small percentage of the community often at the expense of the cultural and information needs of the community as a whole.

Questions about the role and ethics of reference service may change and shift in the years come, but identifying and establishing the true mission of the library may be one way to solve and resolve these questions and issues.

Intellectual Freedom

The development and provision of specific library services and interests is a process that reflects the profession's development and the growth of libraries. New services and professional ideas reflect the societal changes of the times. One of the relatively recent developments in library history is the championing of intellectual freedom. Intellectual freedom, in little more than fifty years, has become one of the basic tenets of the library profession in the United States. When we recently asked a large group of librarians to identify elements of the ALA Code of Professional Ethics, they were able to easily identify two of the eight provisions, the right of patron confidentiality and the concept of intellectual freedom.

While individual members may have had an interest in the issue long before the Association had one, the first Library Bill of Rights was adopted in 1939 and gradually evolved over the years to the current version of the document. The belief that intellectual freedom is a long-standing tradition in library service is commonly held but is not entirely accurate, as the *ALA Intellectual Freedom Manual* states,

> At the outset, two myths can be dispelled, namely, that intellectual freedom in libraries is a tradition, and that intellectual freedom has always been a major, if not the major, part of the foundation of library service in the United States. Both myths, assumed by many librarians, are grounded in the belief that librarians support a static concept of intellectual freedom. Nothing, however, could be further from the truth.[40]

The question then remains, what is the truth about the position of intellectual freedom in the history of the profession? Where did this concept come from, what inspired it, and how did it become one of the most accepted tenets of librarianship in the United States? And how does that history affect librarians today in their understanding and application of the ethics of intellectual freedom, with both traditional materials and electronic resources?

It is not our intent to provide a comprehensive overview of the intellectual freedom movement in the United States. We instead present some theories which explain the development of intellectual freedom as a library concern. We also discuss how intellectual freedom is currently viewed today and how the past and the present may affect the ethical decisions we make regarding intellectual freedom issues in the future.

Censorship within the library was not what inspired the intellectual freedom movement. Since the beginning of the public library movement, librarians have censored and excluded materials for a variety of reasons, including poor writing, inappropriateness for the collection, and moral deficiencies. George Bowerman, former librarian of the Public Library of the District of Columbia, stated in 1908, "If a book, especially a novel, makes evil appear good, by glorifying dishonest acts and principles, if it makes treachery and rascality ideals, it has no proper place in a public circulating library whose privileges are fully open to the young and old."[41] This willingness to censor materials that were not morally uplifting was apparently a comfortable and accepted position for most librarians.

While most contemporary librarians would not phrase their objections with the same language today, a societal backlash against certain kinds of books—those perceived as lacking in redeeming social or moral value—has developed in recent history. The controversy surrounding *American Psycho* by Brett Ellis is an instructive case. The work was to have been published by Simon and Schuster, but was dropped at the last minute, and published later the same year by Random House. The book was boycotted by the National Organization for Women, and *Publishers Weekly* went so far as to publish a list of "Questions and Answers about *American Psycho*" for use by retailers who chose to stock the book, to assist them in handling questions from customers.[42]

Library reaction to *American Psycho* was mixed, but apparently in spite of some positive reviews and the book's appearance on the *New York Times* bestseller list, many librarians chose not to purchase it. In September of 1994 it was reported that only about 400 copies were listed in the OCLC database[43]; in 1996 the figure was 549 copies. This type of self-censorship is common, as was seen in purchasing decisions for Madonna's *Sex*. It is often justified in terms of the cost of materials, collection development policies, and other issues, but the librarian's or the public's perception of the book's moral stance is often a consideration in the nonselection of materials.

So if historically, and even currently, librarians have been willing to live with self-censorship of materials, what woke librarians up and brought them to their current commitment to intellectual freedom? There is obviously more than one cause or reason for the rise of intellectual freedom. Evelyn Geller, in her article "Intellectual Freedom," lays out a variety of approaches to the development of intellectual freedom as a concern for librarians and as a touchstone of library ideology.[44] While no theory can decisively answer the question, the following five theories present unique perspectives on the shift from the acceptability of self-censorship to intellectual freedom.

The first theory: The move to intellectual freedom has been seen by some scholars as part of the general development of the profession of librarianship. Fiske states that the following factors played parts in the shift: the adoption of professional standards to ensure that members have common qualifications and that others are excluded from the profession, the shift on the professional level to discussion of more substantive issues, and the establishment of autonomy for the members of the profession.[45]

Also, as the intellectual freedom movement grew from its beginnings in the 1930s, the belief developed that intellectual freedom is one area in which librarians truly remain experts and authorities. This use of intellectual freedom as an area of professional expertise and authority may also play a part in the contemporary fidelity to the issues of intellectual freedom. The need for a profession to lead in some important area is met by the profession's stand on intellectual freedom and the role library professionals play in the arena of First Amendment rights and the right to read.

The second theory: As we have suggested earlier in this chapter, librarians were often followers and not leaders of society, and the profession's values shifted with societal values. The move from closed to open shelves and the changing attitude toward fiction in libraries may reflect the profession's ability to sense the mood of society and change its mission and values according to new societal norms. The intellectual freedom movement was perhaps also a reaction to the general public's discomfort with the increased level of censorship that began with the start of World War I.

This theory is further refined by those who say that the library served only the cultural and intellectual elite and that librarians followed the shifting mores and values of only that part of society.[46] Did the fact that since the beginning of libraries the majority of library patrons had come from the cultural or societal elite cause librarians to change their views when their primary clientele changed its views and perceptions regarding censorship and intellectual freedom?

The third theory: Presenting a different perspective, Dorothy Broderick portrays the move to intellectual freedom not as a response to society but as a relinquishment of societal responsibility. She proposed that before the 1950s libraries had a "covenant with the community" for the library to be a moral trustee for the public and that the embrace of intellectual freedom was an abandonment of that responsibility in a move toward a more neutral position. Broderick also claims that intellectual freedom came to the fore in American libraries not because books were attacked but because libraries were attacked by the likes of Joseph McCarthy.

In Broderick's view, librarians were not fighting for the printed word or for intellectual freedom but for self-preservation.[47] While developments such as the Library Bill of Rights took place as early as the 1930s, Broderick sees the 1950s attack on libraries as a turning point in the profession's embrace of intellectual freedom. She then raises the question whether contemporary librarians who espouse intellectual freedom have become afraid to make the same moral decisions that their predecessors for years considered part of their professional obligation to the public. This potential abandonment of responsibility puts a very different light on the portrayal of the intellectual freedom champion as the moral crusader.

The fourth theory: Along the same lines as Broderick, Michael Harris sees the move to intellectual freedom and a move to neutrality as a logical progression of a passive profession. Intellectual freedom can be seen as a position of noninvolvement. Harris contends that the librarian has taken the easy way out of any conflict by using intellectual freedom as a justification for not having to make decisions regarding books or social issues. In adopting an intellectual freedom stance, librarians switched from the mission of guidance and selecting material for the patron to the more custodial role of providing all information regardless of moral, political or social view.[48] The problems which arise from this position of neutrality and noninvolvement are discussed later in this chapter.

The fifth theory: Another factor that we believe was an additional influence on the profession's development of intellectual freedom was the increasing imposition of censorship during the 1920s on library materials by outside sources. Most present-day defenders of intellectual freedom decry attacks on the library by outside groups, either individuals or organizations. That type of attack threatens not just the library's collection but also the librarian's right to make informed professional decisions regarding collection development and book selection.

This fear of outside groups' setting library policy and second guessing librarians and their selection of materials is a key part of the intellectual freedom movement. Discussions of self-censorship within the library or even within the publishing profession do not stir the intellectual freedom crusaders as much as outside groups challenging collections. Historically, librarians were willing and able to self-censor materials for a variety of reasons. The threat that the government or private groups or individuals would make decisions regarding library materials provided the catalyst for the Library Bill of Rights and the intellectual freedom movement.

Government involvement with censorship included departments such as the Customs Bureau, the Post Office, and municipal authorities, including the police. Events such as the Customs Bureau's 1928 publication of blacklists of materials not to be allowed into the country, the Post Office's erratic and heavy-handed confiscation of materials it judged to be obscene, and the existence of local censoring agencies such as the police and the New England Watch and Ward Society were signs that groups other than librarians saw themselves in a position to judge what both individuals and libraries should be able to purchase and use.

Censoring groups had existed prior to this time and libraries had worked with organizations such as the New England Watch and Ward Society, which was responsible for censoring materials in Boston. But those groups and others like them censored on behalf of the library and therefore seemed more acceptable than the censorship by agencies the libraries saw as external, arbitrary, and capricious. The activity of these objectionable censoring agencies, along with the controversial changes in writing style and content exemplified by authors such as D.H. Lawrence and James Joyce, brought the issue of censorship to a much wider audience. The library, which for years was content to self-censor material based on its own guidelines and standards, was now forced to assert its right to select and house materials that others thought were pornographic, obscene, or immoral.

While individuals and libraries were struggling to get material that had been censored, the American Library Association was silent on the issue of censorship and intellectual freedom until the late 1930s. At that time a book finally emerged that was censored not for sex, violence, or even immorality but for its social stand: John Steinbeck's *The Grapes of Wrath*. In response to this censorship effort, the ALA wrote and adopted the first Library Bill of Rights in 1939.

All of these theories probably have some truth in them, as contradictory as some of them may seem when taken together. The fact is that changing societal demands, changing professional standards, historical events, and the actions of outside organizations all had an impact on the profession, and the library's role changed accordingly. Acknowledging this allows us to see that the profession's championing of intellectual freedom was not developed out of a single experience or out of a consensus among library professionals. But regardless of its unclear origins, it has nevertheless become a cornerstone of the contemporary library mission.

How firmly this cornerstone will hold in the midst of a technological revolution is a question that cannot yet be answered. The reluctance of some librarians to promote Internet access and the shift in format from text to graphics raises questions regarding the library's abandonment of a moral stance in favor of intellectual freedom. The possibility also exists that in the changing world of librarianship, where some feel that the entire profession is on the brink of extinction, or at least in the throes of radical change, it may be that intellectual freedom is the one arena that still provides the profession with the recognition and leadership that many see as waning in the information age.

The support of the intellectual freedom statement in the professional code of ethics and the endorsement of the Library Bill of Rights are important components of how we define ourselves as a profession and how we present ourselves to the world. Our understanding of the issues surrounding the development of that value can help shape and guide individual decision making.

Neutrality in Information and the Profession

The vision of neutrality also pervades thinking about information, libraries and librarianship. It is a vision because in spite of all attempts at neutrality, whether it be in our professional decisions, the running of the library, or the application of technology, absolute neutrality is not a possibility. All acts, decisions, and events are shaped and formed by the social, political and historical milieu in which they are made.

Even technology which has no heart or soul is not neutral. Nolan Shepard presents Robert Boguslaw's point about neutrality and technology when he states that "Technology is never neutral. It embodies a set of human values often latent, obscure, or deliberately disguised. One of the tasks of well motivated individuals is to expose the precise nature of value choices embodied in various forms of technology."[49] So if even the machines that we create and use embody values and ideas, how can libraries and librarians attain a higher level of neutrality?

Neutrality of course is not just an absolute. Neutrality can be a goal of an institution or a profession even as it acknowledges that the ideal can never be attained. But the importance of acknowledging the factors influencing professional or institutional neutrality are also important. If we know what has influenced us in the past, and what assumptions we are currently operating under, perhaps we can more faithfully work toward the neutrality that evades our good faith efforts.

The image of the library as neutral has perhaps three components: the neutrality of the materials contained in the library, the neutrality of the librarian and the information provided to the patron, and the issue of professional neutrality. The first two issues librarians deal with in the daily work setting when decisions are made regarding purchases, reference questions, and so on. The third is of importance to the profession as a whole and to our views of what our professional organizations should represent.

Historically, it is apparent that at no time in library history have books been perceived as neutral sources of unbiased information. Well known examples include the active self-censorship of librarians as embodied in the fiction problem of the late 1800s, the aggressive anti–German weeding of collections in both world wars, the removal of communist material in the McCarthy era, and the subsequent removal of pro–McCarthy material after he was discredited. Librarians have long acknowledged that individual books have a moral or political stance; a particular title's inclusion in a library collection may be dependent on both the book and the social and political climate. While some discrete pieces of "information" may be neutral, books have always been thought of as tied to the non-neutral position of an author.

The library solution to the fact that books are not neutral cannot be the response, "we just won't have any." Libraries are made up of books or other information sources and so the question of how to ensure neutrality took a different turn. For many the goal of collection development is the achievement of the "balanced collection." In the balanced collection theory, the assumption is that if all sides of an issue are represented by books that are inherently nonneutral, the library can then become a neutral site since each book's position will be balanced by the others. If carried out, this solution would mean that for every book on creationism a book on evolution would be bought. Or perhaps one really good big book on a topic would balance out two smaller and less well known books carrying the opposing view.

For obvious reasons the true "balanced collection" is not possible. The ability to determine a book's political, social or moral stance is difficult. Books just are not labeled that way. Questions also arise over how many viewpoints to represent. What if all the books on evolution are checked out, has the collection then been tipped in favor of creationism? The recognition that moral and political biases are an inherent part of our thinking and writing also make "balance" impossible. While balance may be impossible, the ideal of working toward balance is a value in most libraries. Purchases are made with the knowledge that more than one side of an issue must be represented and that selecting quality books on a broad range of topics may be the closest a library can get to a neutral collection.

The question of the neutrality of the collection also becomes problematic when placed in the context of the values of the community the library serves. Does the library's attempts to achieve neutrality in information take priority over the community or the institution's values and needs? The library may choose to promote the concept of neutrality in spite of a community's objections. The library profession may have embraced a balanced collection but the community may not see the need for representing both sides of the issue if one side is seen as morally wrong. What then is the library's role in pursing an agenda of neutrality in spite of the opposition of the patrons the library is to serve?

The attempt to develop a neutral collection is also not without additional problems, since most libraries rely on materials produced by mainstream publishers. The difficulties of collecting publications from small, independent presses add by default another element of bias to a collection. The publishing industry is governed by concerns and values that may make it difficult for divergent views to receive equal treatment. The difficulty of smaller presses in getting materials reviewed also influences collection decisions since reviews are of major importance to acquisition decisions. So the image of neutrality becomes even more problematic for the library.

John Swan provides comfort to the librarian who bemoans the fact that neutrality cannot be achieved. He states that the heightened awareness of the tension involved in attempting to provide equal access to all ideas will lead to a better selection of books. Ignorance or denial of the issue is not the goal.

"Those who are not aware, who deny the presence of the tension, only conduct their censorship without self examination." [50] Our acknowldgement of our biases puts us in a better position to achieve neutrality.

So if it is not possible for libraries to be truly neutral in the collection of materials perhaps is it more likely that they can be neutral in the provision of service. This kind of neutrality is reflected in two parts of the American Library Association Code of Professional Ethics:

> Section 1: Librarians must provide the highest level of service through appropriate and usefully organized collections, fair and equitable circulation and service policies, and skillful, accurate, *unbiased* and courteous responses to all requests for information.
> Section 7: We distinguish between our personal convictions and professional duties and do not allow our personal beliefs to interfere with fair representations of the aims of our institutions or the provision of access to their information resources[51][italics added].

If we acknowledge the authority of the American Library Association to provide an ethical code (similar statements are in the ethical codes of the Library Association, the Canadian Library Association and the Australian Library Association) it appears that the stated ethical goal of the profession is the neutral, unbiased provision of library service to all patrons. This type of unbiased and nonjudgmental service is the norm in American libraries.

An adherence to neutrality is a major component of what D.J. Foskett, in his work *The Creed of a Librarian* proposed. Foskett states that "If he [a librarian] has no politics, no religion, and no morals, he can have all politics, all religions and all morals."[52] This statement by itself implies ultimate neutrality. The librarian is a blank slate free of all biases, prejudices and opinions in order to best serve the patron.

While this is the traditional view of Foskett's work it should not be taken in isolation from the rest of the chapter in which it appears. Foskett immediately goes on to say that this creed does not mean that librarians *should* not have strong personal feelings about issues; in fact, he says that they should have strong opinions in order to better relate to the patron. His caveat is, then, that those feelings should be put aside when the librarian becomes personally involved with each patron. Strong personal feelings allow librarians to relate to their patrons and the negation of those feelings allows them to better serve those patrons.

Foskett then tempers his statement once more by saying that the librarian should not, in a zeal to identify with the patron, abandon objectivity. The librarian's knowledge and background provide the broad view of the subject that the patron may lack. So the statement—his book's subtitle—"No politics, no religion, and no morals" can now be seen in a different light. Librarians may be neutral in deciding not to impose their views on the patron but they are also in a position to attempt to introduce the reader to a wider range of information than they may request. Does that requirement negate the neutrality that was established by the first directive? Is neutrality maintained when alternative views are presented to a patron who did not request them? For many the answer would be yes, the willingness of the librarian to answer all questions and to take at face value the interests and needs of the patron, and to provide them with a wide range of information sources, may be as close to neutral service as is possible.

Foskett's admonition to bring a wide range of information to the patron and to perhaps broaden their perspective is not the same as forcing a personal opinion on the patron. Foskett's view may be then seen as that of the neutral librarian providing a range of nonneutral information to the patron. That form of neutrality should perhaps be the goal that reference work is measured by. This view also retains the professionalism of the librarian, because it is the professional responsibility of all librarians to provide information and also to use their skills and knowledge to provide the best and broadest range of information that is possible. Attempts at complete neutrality could be considered an abdication of the librarian's professional responsibility to the patron.

A completely neutral stance, such as the statement "no politics, no religion no morals," is what is decried by Hauptman in his bomb experiment.[53] It is this type of reference service that treats all information requests as neutral that Hauptman finds inexcusable. Hauptman proposes that the librarian has a moral obligation not to remain neutral when faced with a question that they find morally suspect. He feels that the individual's responsibility to themselves would take precedence over their professional responsibility to the patron. The potential would therefore arise that the librarian would have to judge each question for its agreement or disagreement with their own ethical views prior to answering a question. For many this view of the librarian as a moral judge is not an acceptable one; for them the professional stance should be founded on some agreed-upon interpretation of Foskett's view of neutrality.

A different view of the neutrality issue in the provision of service is seen in the proposal of Gillian Gremmels which was briefly discusses in the Introduction to the present work. Gremmels dismisses the idea that objectivity is possible when she states: "The untenability of objectivity as a foundation for thought or practice calls the traditional hands-off approach to reference ethics into question."[54] This thought does not lead her, as it might Hauptman, to then infer that if neutrality is not possible, and issues of morality are involved, then the librarian should make decisions or recommendations based on a personal system of morals. Gremmels instead attempts to apply a theory of communitarian ethics to librarianship.

This theory would place the public interest over either the information needs of the individual or the personal morals of the librarian. This approach requires the acceptance, by librarians and the public, of the concept that librarians, either collectively or individually, are able to arrive at a consensus about what is truly the public interest. The possibility of confusing public interest with private morals is a dilemma, as is the potentially arbitrary application of the theory based solely on the reference interview and an individual's interpretation of the reference question.

Gremmel's view does offer us a framework for making judgments at the reference desk that is sorely lacking in discussions about reference and information neutrality. While the theory may not be widely accepted, it does pose a way of dealing with the neutrality question. This acknowledgment of the complexity of the issue is seldom seen in the professional literature. Too often the issue of neutrality is only brought into the discussion when issues involving professional neutrality are raised. Debates periodically rage over whether the profession should take a stand on a given issue or attempt to maintain professional neutrality by noninvolvement in political and social issues. These types of discussions have been regular features in the library literature and at American Library Association Council and Membership meetings for the last thirty years.

While it must be acknowledged that there is no one unified voice for the profession, the activities and stance of the American Library Association make it the obvious example to use as we discuss the issue of professional neutrality.

As stated earlier in the chapter, the ALA has historically not been an active voice in social or political issues, with major exceptions being the involvement in and activities surrounding World War I and World War II. With the exception of lone voices, there was no outrage from the profession over the segregation of black libraries or the discrimination against black librarians, no statement regarding the rights of women to vote or other civil right issues of the twentieth century, the ERA being a notable exception. The profession was unwilling or unable to take stands that were contrary to the conservative views of the society as a whole. This avoidance of involvement with contemporary social problems presented to the world, depending upon your point of view, a stance of reasoned neutrality or an abdication of moral leadership.

As societal concerns and values began changing in the 1960s so did the concerns of some in the Association. The emergence of socially active groups within the Association reflected the concerns and values of social activists outside the profession. The conflicts which arose from discussions of social issues were a reflection of the times. It is not a surprise that librarianship reflects the culture of which it is a part; some, such as Michael Harris, feel however, that the profession has always re-acted to those external, social and political cues and has not developed the strength and integrity of purpose that would allow it to be on the vanguard of social or political change.[55]

This lack of an internally developed sense of professionalism and basic values can be seen as an element in the neutrality debates of the profession.

Since there was no internal moral voice, the stage was set for heated debate about the role of the profession in social issues.

So when the profession did attempt to make statements regarding social issues, it became a profession divided. For some the concept of the profession making statements regarding social or political issues was a direct violation of the Library Bill of Rights and the ALA Constitution. David Berninghausen in his article "Social Responsibility vs. The Library Bill of Rights" presents the argument that no matter how important or relevant are issues such as racial justice, peace, the separation of church and state, or any other of a host of others, "it is not the purpose of ALA to take positions on how men must resolve them."[56] This approach is based on the necessity of complete neutrality for information and libraries.

Berninghausen makes the argument that since we really cannot know what the truth is, how can we make decisions about social issues or presume to say what is good, or just, or moral? He then uses the ALA Library Bill of Rights as a defense against taking any stance, making the assumption that if the Association takes a stand on an issue, libraries will naturally then vigorously weed or build their collections to be in accordance. This type of action would then lead to censorship and be a violation of the Library Bill of Rights.

This article was published in *Library Journal* in November 1972 and in January 1973 that periodical published nineteen essays written in response to it. While some authors vigorously supported Berninghausen's rationale there were others who took the author to task for not looking at other reasons for social involvement of the profession. Betty-Carol Sellen wrote that involvement with social responsibility is a response to the imbalance of library service, that conservative issues have long since been supported in libraries, and that under-represented ideals and groups need to have the same representation.[57] Jane Robbins claimed that "The library is not an institution which exists removed from our increasingly interdependent and politicized world. The professionals who control American's information institutions ... cannot retreat into those institutions and ignore the larger society. The result of this sort of myopic professionalism is to support intellectual freedom for those who have power while denying it to those who are powerless."[58] Other writers stated similar ideas, such as, "librarians have the obligation to join the democratic forum as librarians, and would be remiss if their profession failed to make its contribution."[59]

So for some, such as Berninghausen, the attempt to remain neutral on all social and political issues is the only way to retain our professional status and responsibility. For others the lack of concern about social and political issues is an abdication of our professional responsibility. This conflict has been played out on the Association level many times since the Berninghausen debates in 1972 and 1973. The Israeli Censorship Resolution passed by Membership in 1992 and revoked by ALA Council in 1993 again raised anxieties over the issue of professional neutrality on social and political issues and once again a flurry of writings appeared in the pages of the library press regarding the role of the Association and of the profession in these areas. These ongoing and often acrimonious debates serve to point out the complexity of the profession's views regarding professional neutrality.

Libraries are integral parts of the communities in which they serve, and those communities and constituents are daily faced with an enormous number of social and political issues affecting not only the individuals and the community but also the library. The concept of professional neutrality in the face of these issues becomes more difficult to defend if we accept two premises: (1) information is not neutral and (2) libraries have traditionally responded to the lead and norms of the mainstream, relatively conservative American culture.

If information is not neutral, if moral judgments are a part of information usage, and if one of our jobs as a profession is to recognize those judgments and make decisions, it would seem that certain principles of truth, justice, equality, and freedom must be defining values for the profession. If we are unable or unwilling to state those values in a public forum, then how can we expect our patrons to honor and respect those values? We may also have to make statements in opposition to the views of mainstream American political views. It is foreseeable that the concept of intellectual freedom, both in print and electronically, will again be at the fore of American politics. The profession has publicly stated that intellectual freedom is a value we care about and a political ideal we feel we need to pursue as a profession, even if it is an ideal challenged by many other Americans. Will we respond to the mainstream by changing our values?

The question of neutrality is not an easy one for the individual librarian or the profession as a whole. More discussion is needed on what it means to say that information is neutral and what the ramifications are in acknowledging that information can have moral value.

Chapter 4

Resolving Ethical Problems in Librarianship

Librarianship stands at a crossroads. No single decision will determine its future, but in the absence of self-conscious and critical reflection, the course of the profession will be charted by larger social forces which may or may not further the highest goals of the librarian. Our strategy in the present study has been to understand those goals, first, by laying down a foundation in the form of an analysis of the moral value of information, and second, by looking for the current understanding of the profession in its professional codes and organizational structure.

We then argued that librarians must articulate their mission more directly and redesign their work organizations to fit their understanding of who they are professionally. We also wrote about how crucial information was to moral development and yet how cautious librarians are to define their mission in terms of a positive duty to promote information and critical thinking. Finally, we discussed some of the choices librarians need to make about how their professional identity is reflected in their work organizations. If librarians need to exercise autonomous judgment in defining and evaluating their work, their work organizations should not be structured like fifties era command and control hierarchies.

Our historical review of the public library movement put the results of the first two chapters in motion by showing how clarity and confusion in library history go together with insights and oversights about the mission of the librarian. Over and again we have seen that "new" challenges to the profession were really the resurfacing of old ambivalences and unsettled business. Where history repeats itself, we can often find the same unsettled questions emerging in different contexts. Are librarians educators? Moral arbiters? Custodians of the community's cultural center? Even if there are no final answers to these questions, the quality of our thinking about them will determine our ability to handle novel formulations of the three contending missions.

125

As we turn to present-day issues for a practical application of our thinking about information ethics and professional ethics, we also develop a picture of the information age librarian. That picture is sketched as part of a general conclusion in Chapter 5, but in the present chapter we want it to emerge through a series of concrete choices we think information age librarians should embrace.

We have chosen three general headings for locating specific, mission-defining ethical issues: neutrality, collections, and service. Since the naturalness of these headings may not be immediately apparent, something should be said about why we see the ethical problems of librarianship organized under them. After all, the subject headings one finds in library ethics literature follow more closely the major divisions of professional library work (e.g., reference ethics, cataloging ethics, library management ethics).

"Collecting" and "serving" seem to us so basic to the nature of librarianship that no redescription of professional mission would leave them behind. Even if the "cyber library" becomes a reality and physical collections become less central, we will still think of librarians as people who collect and manage points of access to knowledge, information, and culture. Likewise, almost all libraries serve patrons, whether through face-to-face encounters or through the mediation of a catalog, index, or online service.

When we selected concrete issues to discuss and resolve, we initially came up with a fairly standard set of topical concerns: Internet access, technology in reference services, the reference interview, technology in cataloging, the "fee or free" debate, and current controversies about "balance" and "family values" in collections. These are, indeed, some of the hottest and most "mission-sensitive" issues in librarianship. But when treated as a series of discrete ethical brushfires in the landscape of librarianship, they still seemed hard to compass or control.

The various solutions to these problems seem to turn on diverse ways of thinking about what librarians are doing when they collect information and what their service mission is. In both areas we found ourselves returning to questions and assumptions about neutrality, so we decided to discuss the general problem of neutrality as a professional obligation and use some of the results of that discussion to develop a philosophical and practical position on collections and service.

Process Approaches to Professional Ethics Cases

One's natural reaction to an ethical problem is to try to solve it by making a direct judgment about the issue at hand. This seems such a sensible approach that it is hard to imagine any other way of handling ethical problems.

Whether the problem comes to us through our direct experience, or a friend or colleague, or a third party such as a newspaper article or journal article, if we care about it at all, we typically assume the role of judge and jury and make some kind of judgment. We could call this the "juridical model" for handling ethical issues.

In spite of this tendency, most of us are also aware that many moral problems, especially those which arise in professional practice, depend for their solution on consultations with a variety of affected and interested parties. "Doing justice" to others and showing them moral respect usually require us to avoid making hasty assumptions about what their moral interest is in a given situation. We show that we know this when, in the course of trying to solve complex moral problems, we ask probing questions about the intention and goals of various parties to the problem. We may be no less willing to render a judgment in such cases, but we appreciate that some of the variables lie outside our knowledge.

To see the distinctive feature of a "process" solution to an ethical problem, one need only go one step further by recognizing sometimes that not only do we need more information about the people involved in the problem, but we must actually solve the problem by appealing to a process requiring their active involvement. The most obvious examples of process approaches to problems in professional life are due process procedures, especially those followed for handling complaints, hiring, promotion, and firing decisions. In these cases the juridical model breaks down, often because the complainant alleges that the person or group who made an initial judgment failed to be objective in some way. When organizations use "due process" procedures to appeal allegedly unjust judgements they are often substituting a process model of deliberation for a juridical model.

The distinctive feature of a process model of ethical deliberation is that it treats the "moral" resolution of a problem as the one which emerges from a well defined and faithfully followed process. As in due process, procedural ethical deliberation is itself modeled on the procedural justice of the criminal and civil justice system. Rather than look for one wise and objective person to decide all cases in the justice system, we establish an elaborate set of rules and procedures which, if followed, define for anyone a just outcome. Likewise, some moral problems do not seem to have universal and uncontroversial solutions. In those cases one might decide that, even if we do not know in advance the right outcome for the problem, we do know what process will find the best outcome.

Process ethics will seem counterintuitive to many. How can we know what the right process is, and know what it means to follow that process in the right manner, and yet not know what the actual outcome is? Again, the analogy to procedural justice in the criminal justice system might help. In the course of a criminal proceeding, two crucial events occur which have bearing on process ethics. The first is "discovery," the process of bringing to light facts and testimony relevant to the case. The second is the more subtle "representation" of the parties in the process—the involvement, with understanding, of various parties with an interest in the proceeding.

To see what difference process ethics can make in the moral experience of a professional librarian, consider the following two ways of resolving a moral problem. Suppose that one or more reference librarians at a public library are concerned that, because of budgetary pressures, they are forced to have increasingly superficial interactions with patrons. They raise this issue with the senior reference librarian.

The supervisor who follows a substantive (or, juridical) approach to the problem will do some of the following things: observe reference desk service, discuss the problem with reference librarians, compare service standards with other libraries, survey patrons, make a professional judgment about the adequacy of the current reference service, and make recommendations to reference librarians.

The supervisor using a process approach may also take some of these steps, but will, in addition, frame the problem within an agreement with reference librarians about the best process to follow for deliberating on the problem, involve reference librarians in that process to the extent they feel they need to be involved, and pursue the outcomes. Notice that these two approaches could conceivably reach the same substantive outcome. What, then, is the moral difference between them?

In spite of the fact that both approaches involved "gathering information," the process approach used a process of discovery that was not bounded by one investigator's judgment. (Consider the difference between a criminal justice system in which the judge conducts discovery for both defense and prosecution and the American system with a largely adversarial process of discovery.) Also, in the process approach the professionals who experience moral concern about whether they are satisfying their professional obligations also experience the deliberation of that concern. Not only is their practical "ownership" of the outcome greater, but their intrinsic interest in the problem has been respected—a significant moral difference. We might say that they have experienced "moral representation" in the problem.

Thus, process ethics will only seem counterintuitive if one thinks that the involvement of individuals in moral deliberation is purely of instrumental value to securing a "moral" outcome. If one feels, however, that moral outcomes sometimes depend upon the actual involvement of individuals in deliberation, perhaps because such involvement reduces alienation and develops personal autonomy, then process ethics will sometimes make a moral difference. Also, it should be pointed out that the process of discovery in process ethics models can, potentially, produce better information because it is not bounded by the skills and perspectives of a single investigator.

One can see that a process approach to a moral problem might make sense in situations in which (a) there is great uncertainty or reasonable difference of opinion about the best outcome or solution; (b) the kinds and sources of information relevant to the solution are complex and include "testimony" of professional experience; (c) the involvement of various parties to the problem will likely make a moral difference to them; (d) the solution involves tailoring abstract ethical principles to local situations; and (e) the context for the problem is changing and will need to be revisited periodically.

If we think about how these criteria apply to contemporary librarianship, we will see that many professional ethics issues in librarianship have a process dimension. There is great uncertainty about what the professional mission of librarians is in the rapidly changing atmosphere of the information age. Most librarians agree about very general ideals and principles, and many understand that those values need to be adapted to local circumstances. Also, while some ethical issues in librarianship are technical and can be defined in terms of quantitative differences for patrons, many are qualitatively rich and depend for their solution upon discussions among librarians of their experiences with patrons.

There are, however, some problems with the process approach to professional ethics. Like the criminal justice system, process ethics is costly and time consuming. One merely has to calculate the salary costs of a one hour meeting of ten professionals to appreciate how costly it may be to submit problems to a process approach. Certainly, sophistication in the way such joint deliberation is instituted will be crucial to making this approach work. Also, process approaches to ethical problems raise some difficult management issues. Obviously, collective discovery and deliberation depend upon an atmosphere of trust and the absence of fear.

Finally, we can take process ethics too far if we open up deliberation on too many core professional values at once. The stability of a professional working group depends upon agreement about some core values. In discussing concrete ethical problems in the pages which follow, we make substantive judgments about many of them. We also suggest scenarios in which the use of process ethics is warranted. We believe that it is crucial for professionals to pursue two virtues which may, at first glance, seem contradictory: to develop principled convictions about professional values and to remain flexible enough to rethink those convictions in deliberation with others. While these virtues pull us, psychologically, in different directions, their joint realization is crucial to creating a professional work atmosphere which is inclusive and responsive.

Neutrality, Again

Time and again the study of the moral mission of librarianship confronts the question of what it means to say that librarians observe a respectful neutrality with regard to the patron's information needs. Historically, the events which led to the Library Bill of Rights and the most recent American Library Association Code of Ethics seem to have carved out a definite position on neutrality. Librarians are for "free access" and against "censorship"; they are against "bias" and in favor of "presenting all points of view." Above all else, they are against letting groups outside the profession dictate collection decisions or censor library materials.

One might characterize the current understanding of professional neutrality in librarianship as a "vigilant passivity" because the professional consensus reflected in the documents just cited is vigilant in its resistance to obvious threats to free inquiry, yet passive with respect to a positive vision of what inquiry is.

The contemporary understanding of neutrality in librarianship has both theoretical flaws and practical shortcomings. As discussed in the Introduction, value neutrality is an illusory ideal given the interpretive character of knowledge. Chapter 3 documented other theoretical and practical problems with neutrality. Of course, librarians can still see themselves as passive bystanders in the relationship between their patrons and the collective biases of the culture industry, knowledge industry, and publishing industry which work together to fill library shelves. But taken to its logical extreme, such a position neutralizes the importance and legitimate judgment of the librarian.

An internal incoherence was seen in the neutrality thesis. Librarians try to be neutral because they believe in a host of other values: the importance of free speech, intellectual inquiry, cultural experience, critical thinking. But they are not neutral with respect to those values. How does one advocate neutrality while adhering to a substantive vision of inquiry? This tension, if it is not always an incoherence, engenders paradoxes in both collections and service, as is seen in some detail in the next two sections.

How can we move beyond the current understanding of neutrality in librarianship? The first step seems to be an acknowledgment that there are several kinds of neutrality, each of which might be appropriate to promoting specific aspects of professional mission in specific cases. We can all think of many different ways in which librarians could be harmfully biased, but it is interesting that library literature on intellectual freedom and neutrality does not acknowledge the diverse ways of being neutral. Several of these ways are described below, followed by an exploration of some dimensions of the mission of the librarian, with the intention of correlating different kinds of neutrality with different aspects of mission.

Neutrality in patron service could mean either "outcome-neutrality" or "process-neutrality." Professional librarians can hardly be expected to be neutral with respect to the processes one might follow to pursue an inquiry. After extensive training in reference and review sources, librarians should be prepared to make informed decisions about the best ways of pursuing a question. On the other hand, normally it is not appropriate to have in mind a particular outcome or result for the inquiry and then lead the patron to it.

If one has a commitment to a particular school of economics and guides the patron to sources which overrepresent the importance of that school of thought, then one has clearly done the patron a disservice. Notice, however, that it is not merely outcome nonneutrality that causes harm in these cases, but the combination of outcome and process nonneutrality. Many cases of outcome bias could be resolved by a faith in a legitimate process of inquiry. The greater the integrity of the process of a given inquiry, the less a librarian should worry about his or her own nonneutrality about the outcome of the inquiry.

When we say that someone is obliged to be neutral or impartial with respect to some outcome or process, we usually mean that the person must "put out of play" their view on the subject. But an important distinction must be made between excluding one's personal convictions and excluding one's knowledge, even though one hopes that there is a substantial overlap between the two.

Consider the famous "Dowd" experiment in which the "patron" asks for information on free basing cocaine. Does neutrality require suppression of the librarian's personal conviction that drug use is immoral, as well as their knowledge that free-basing cocaine is harmful? Most librarians would say that neutrality requires suppression of both convictions. After all, neither was part of the patron's inquiry.

We rightly worry that librarians who too freely express their views and convictions to patrons will have a "chilling effect" on their patron's inquiries. But we should also worry that librarians who respond too narrowly to explicit requests are denying their patrons an opportunity to consider related aspects of a topic. Neutrality should not normally prevent librarians from raising collateral issues and inquiry opportunities for the patron to consider.

To what extent does neutrality bar the representation of "background knowledge" which the librarian may claim to have? On the one hand, the librarian is not likely to be a subject expert, so he or she may be reluctant to present background knowledge directly to the patron. On the other hand, inquiry is not merely a skill in using authorities, but also an ability to make inferences from background knowledge to fruitful avenues of research. In putting backgroung knowledge "out of play," the librarian's worries about bias may lead to advancing a view of neutrality which is inconsistent with high quality inquiry! One could say that it is the patron's job to make such inferences, but sometimes such background knowledge is precisely what the patron lacks.

The tensions raised by the pursuit of neutrality are also endemic to other educational contexts. Teachers are both content experts and coaches to their student's inquiry. When expertise is called for, there is no question of being neutral. One claims to know the state of opinion or knowledge on a subject, which implies a degree of confidence about one's claims and suspicion about contrary views. However, in many cases, the goal of teaching inquiry skills (or teaching more subtle lessons) requires what might be called "strategic neutrality," a temporary holding in abeyance of one's conviction for the purpose of motivating independent thinking and inquiry in the student. Finally, there are times when nonneutrality can be productive in leading inquiry. By "confessing" a bias, one can help students see what is at stake for you in a subject, without shutting down their own process of reflection.

All of these uses of neutrality and nonneutrality are well known to teachers. What is surprising about library discussions of neutrality is that they conceive of the various contexts for education in the library setting as less diverse and more restricted than the classroom educational setting. The opposite is true; there are at least as many situations in which the librarian can fulfill their educational mission by making use of neutrality and nonneutrality.

Why have discussions of neutrality in librarianship not more closely paralleled thinking about neutrality in other educational settings? There are several reasonable answers. First, the intellectual freedom movement had a different impact on libraries than on teachers. Ironically, in the case of teachers, intellectual freedom involves protecting the free inquiry and expressed convictions of the teacher from adverse treatment from employers, whereas in the case of librarianship, intellectual freedom, in the doctrine of neutrality, led to protection of the patron from the pressure of outside groups and the views of librarians.

Second, public librarians are "public servants" and are held to standards of neutrality similar to other public workers. Academic librarians' roles are still thought of as ancillary to classroom education, thus their personae as teachers remain underdeveloped. Finally, the gender-specific history of the library profession, should not be ignored. As participants in "women's work," librarians of the past took on some of the cultural expectations of women's behavior in the domestic sphere: passivity, self-effacement, and servility.[1]

So far neutrality has been discussed in its most common practical connection, reference service. But neutrality also governs librarians' perceptions of their role in civic life. As with other intellectuals and public advocates, librarians are well situated to take a professional interest in information-related issues in their communities. When library programs address local issues, however, controversy is often the result. The public is not yet used to the idea that librarians have various kinds of expertise which qualify them to take professional interest in local issues. Similarly, academic libraries unevenly grant faculty status to librarians, showing an ambivalence about their role as researchers and professional educators.

Minimally, librarians should be invited to gather, present, and discuss resources which help people think through contemporary controversy and political issues. Librarians are also well suited to be curators of a community's cultural experience and identity, providing a kind of "applied ethnology" for the library's service area. Doubtless, such activity will stir controversy, but a legacy of the neutrality issue is that the controversy revolves around whether librarians should be involved in such activities at all. In keeping librarians "neutral," communities deny themselves the use of some of their best guides to issues. Paradoxical as it may sound, if librarians are serious about the values that have led them to pursue an ideal of neutrality—the values of inquiry and rich cultural experience—then they must design their professional practices to actively (and non-neutrally) reflect those values.

So far we have been advocating a more complex approach to neutrality, one which gives librarians much greater latitude in the ways that they become involved in their patron's and community's information needs. But we have skirted the most serious objection to moving away from neutrality: the possibility, indeed likelihood, that individuals will be self-deceived about the "reasonableness" of their non-neutral service. While there are good reasons for librarians to spend more time getting to know their patrons' inquiry needs and to devote more creative energy to assessing their community's needs, unwanted is a revival of the stereotype of the imperious and scolding librarian who takes liberties to impose irrelevant rules and proprieties on the patron.

Having kept outside groups from dictating collections policy, the profession would not want to encourage politically radical or religiously zealous librarians to substitute their preferences for the considered judgment of a professional staff. In asking librarians to become less anonymous to patrons, to develop and become known in their community for specific areas of expertise, we need to remember that most people tend to overestimate their objectivity and underestimate the inhibiting effects of their personality on others. We may want to abandon the myth of "professional objectivity," but it may be preferable to the reality of unrestrained subjectivity.

This problem is ripe for a process ethics solution. Once librarians begin to acknowledge that they are not neutral, they can begin to discuss candidly the appropriateness of expressing specific values in specific decisions. As long as librarians associate professional practice with the mythic ideal of neutrality, they will view their experiences of value conflicts as professional failings instead of natural and potentially beneficial opportunities. It is crucial, however, that a process for discussing experiences of nonneutrality be established.

In university teaching, for example, where there is still some leisure to work, faculty frequently talk about how to engage students in value rich inquiry without the negative consequences mentioned above. While the process for checking intuitions about the appropriate use of values in interactions with students is somewhat informal, faculty have ample opportunity to discuss actual incidents and hypothetical cases with colleagues. Librarians need a similar process for gathering and comparing their thinking about how to both balance and express values in collections and services. The sections which follow consider more specific issues in each of these areas.

Collection Development

Frustration abounds in most works on library ethics in that while much information is given, there are usually very few solutions offered to daily problems. This lack of answers is not surprising; every situation and environment is unique and no solution can work for all libraries. But the lack of answers may also be an example of the profession's reluctance to move away from traditional thinking. So, while it would be presumptuous to dictate ethical solutions for others, we feel there is also a need to be able to articulate how librarians might arrive at decisions regarding some of the major issues they face. These approaches may be simplistic in nature or, indeed, for some, just plain wrong but they represent a synthesis of the concepts presented in the preceding chapters and may be used as a springboard for organizational or professional discussions of ethical problems.

Collection development—which may be defined as the collection of print, nonprint and electronic resources—is the traditional core of the library. Without a collection the traditional library would not exist. How that collection is acquired, developed, cataloged, and preserved are key questions facing librarians. Three problem areas in collection development are dealt with in the following text: the role of the community and interest groups in collection development versus the role of the library professional; how librarians deal with their increasing lack of control over collections and the contents of the collection, especially regarding electronic resources; and the concern over providing Internet access.

All libraries operate within a geographic and organizational setting. The library has been established to serve a defined group of people who support the library with tax dollars, tuition dollars, or perhaps earnings from a company. These users form one of many interrelated groups that are the library stakeholders. Other stakeholders include staff, management, governing boards, and trustees. All of these groups have an interest in determining the mission and the purpose of the library.

Some of these public constituency groups also see themselves as having a role to play in the development of library policy and perhaps even the administration of the library in such areas as collection development and public services, roles that have traditionally been reserved for library staff. Challenges to library materials or library policies often place constituency groups, some large, some small, in direct conflict with the professional judgment of the library staff.

These conflicts come in the form of censorship challenges, the request to add additional materials to the collection, the felt need to impose limits and restrictions on use of materials or services such as the Internet. These conflicts can be attributed to a variety of causes: the desire of a group to impose their wishes on the community as a whole, the passive nature of the library itself which leaves it open to attacks from the outside, and perhaps most importantly the inability of librarians to articulate the vision and mission of the library.

When there is conflict or confusion over the role of the library various groups will feel free to assume that their, potentially narrow, view of the library's mission is the same as the view of all other groups the library serves.

The vision of a librarian who is in complete control of the collection has changed over the last century. The concern of the librarians of the late 1800s was for the moral character and usefulness of each individual book. The librarian's responsibility was to know the collection and if that included reading each book, so much the better. Book selections were made out of standard sources like the *Fiction Catalog,* which offered conservative, censored lists. The periodicals collection was small, indexed with a single index, and well known to the library staff. Within this environment the librarian could, and did, vouch for the reliability, usefulness, and moral acceptability of each item.

Most contemporary librarians cannot claim the same knowledge of their collections. Subject specialists may have a good grasp of their subject areas but with the increasing number of books in most collections it is unlikely that any one person, even a subject area expert, could claim a knowledge of the book collection. The increased number of periodical titles and the availability of information resources on the Internet make it virtually impossible for the librarian nowadays to maintain more than a superficial knowledge of the contents of the entire collection.

Fortunately, a personal lack of indepth knowledge of the collection is not a hindrance to providing good reference service since there are improved finding tools such as electronic indexes, online catalogs, large bibliographic utilities and various web browsers. While personal knowledge of each item in the collection is impossible, library collections are, through technological advances, almost certainly more accessible to the public in the 1990s than in previous decades. What has been lost is the ability of the librarian to vouch for the intellectual and moral content of each item in the collection.

When constituency groups crusade for the removal, segregation or labeling of books, they often ignore the problems that come with a large, wide-ranging collection. In 1954 the state of Alabama passed a law calling for the labeling of all books used in the state for education purposes as to (1) whether the author is or is not or ever was a member of the Communist party, and (2) whether he or she was or is a "known advocate or member of any Communist-front organization listed by the Attorney General of the United States or Congress or any committee of Congress." The law also stated that this information was to be provided on authors cited in such books. Estimates were made that in one large library in the state a quarter of the collection would be involved, and it would take staff pasting in 300 labels a day to get the project done in a year.[2] The law was declared unconstitutional the same year it was passed.

In 1995, four decades later, a similar bill was introduced in the state of Washington which would have required librarians to segregate all materials with homosexual themes or characters. The Washington law targeted a different "enemy" but revived the same intellectual freedom and logistical nightmare.

These proposals are based not only on the assumption that they could pass intellectual freedom challenges, but that they are logistically feasible. In actuality neither the Alabama nor the Washington proposed requirement, nor any like them, could be met without the expenditure of enormous hours of staff time and even then would entail splitting periodical collections and volumes of encyclopedias and severely limiting Internet access. The modern library has evolved beyond the point of manipulation of the collection to achieve political or moral goals.

The availability of Internet access intensifies the dilemmas faced by collection development. Internet services provide yet another large, uncontrolled, unregulated collection of resources. While the Internet can be seen as just another information source, it is also different in that unlike the traditional materials collected by the library no selection decisions have been made with regard to the bulk of its content. Even though the librarian may not be familiar with all the books and periodicals in the collection, the knowledge that they were acquired in accordance with collection development policies offers the comforting implication that some criteria were used in the selection process. Internet resources have no such guarantee; there are no selection decisions taking place, yet the librarian is put in the position of trying to determine whether they can legitimately deselect certain sites or themes.

The deselection process is fraught with difficulties. Deselection on the Internet is seen by many as censorship, a usurpation of individual responsibility for one's own information needs. Can any attempt at deselection be done without excluding items that may be relevant or necessary for the community? Is deselection even possible from a technological standpoint? Given these obstacles, is deselection a viable strategy for Internet resources management? We believe the answer to this question at present is no.

This forces a more fundamental question: Since Internet information services cannot be managed through traditional collections policy, should these resources be excluded from the library? The answer to that is also no: While

the Internet may not be the capstone of the information age, it is a fast growing, increasingly powerful tool in acquiring and identifying information sources
and a number of patrons will need and require access to the information that
it provides.

So if it is impossible to control the Internet, and perhaps irresponsible to
deny Internet access to patrons, the other solution to the problem of nonse-
lected information is to restrict access to it. Those who would restrict access
use arguments similar to those used for many years to restrict access to adult
material by children. The restrictions are being done to "protect" the child from
potentially immoral or suspicious literature. This type of restriction, based
solely on chronological age, would appear to be in direct violation of the
Library Bill of Rights and its various interpretations, a battle that has already
been fought.[3] While some may argue that there are inherent differences
between the Internet and traditional library resources, the arguments against
age restrictions are still valid with any technology.

In the face of these challenges, how does the librarian deal with the problems of collection development and Internet access? If we did not believe that
there was a moral value attached to information, the problem would be less
troublesome; if information were truly neutral, it would not matter which people had access to it or what uses they put it to. But if we believe that information can have a moral value, how do we justify providing access to materials that may be harmful?

One answer lies in the reevaluation of the mission of the library and the
role of the librarian. One of the historic missions of the library discussed in
Chapter 3 was that of education. Education was the library's most universal
mission and is still reflected in many public library mission statements. It
remains the core mission for academic libraries. Perhaps it is time to see what
librarians as educators can do to better equip their patrons to face the growing collections and variety of information sources currently available to them.

If librarians again take on the mantle of educator, their role will change;
time will be given to the training of patrons in the evaluation of both retrieval
tools and the information obtained. Information will not be provided without ensuring that the patron understands where the information is coming from
and by what measures it should be judged. This type of orientation places the
librarian more in the role of guide and consultant than gatekeeper. It becomes
the librarian's responsibility to determine an individual's information needs
and then to develop a plan which would encompass a wide variety of information sources and to allow for the subsequent involvement with the patron
in the evaluation and implementation of the plan.

While parts of this education role may be familiar to librarians, the application of it to the majority of questions answered would require a major
rethinking of the idea of reference, both on the part of the librarian and on
the part of the patron.

While there is very little information on what the public truly thinks about the role of the library, there is some evidence for us to examine regarding librarians' visions of the role of the library. The role of educator certainly has an historical precedent and is still seen by many librarians as the prime objective of the library. The public may also see education as one of the library's roles but needs to be aware that its potential enhancement as a focus of the library stands in contradiction to the traditional role of the library as moral arbiter for the community.

It was earlier suggested that while the library community has, over the course of the last fifty years of the intellectual freedom movement, relinquished the role of moral arbiter, it is unclear whether the community has. Most local communities probably still consider the library and the library staff responsible for the moral content of the materials that they provide. This makes it easier to understand why issues of censorship and restrictions are so intractable. If the librarian is no longer responsible for the morals of the community or the individual patron, there is a very different set of expectations from the community and a different role for the library. It appears that too often the level of moral responsibility that the community places on the library is more extreme than the library can accept.

Can the community come to see the library as an educational institution that has no obligation to police the community's morals? What can the library offer in place of that vision? The concept of the library as the information provider for the community may well meet that need. The library should become the place that analyzes and recognizes the information needs of the community, helps the community identify its needs, and helps patrons meet their needs.

If librarians are no longer the "moral police" of the community, neither are they amoral custodians of an increasingly "immoral" collection. Libraries should continue to make morally significant judgments about the value of various potential resources. In fact, librarians should be urged to move away from any pretense of neutrality about the moral importance of that aspect of their mission. But the reality is that the heterogeneity of communities in North America and the loss of a truly shared religious or cultural identity make it impossible for the library to meet the information needs of the entire community *and* remain a place that espouses a particular set of moral principles to the exclusion of others. When the profession adopted a stance of intellectual freedom, it ended the role of moral custodian; it appears, however, that we forgot to tell some of our constituent groups, and they are still surprised by the inevitable consequences.

The professional move to a more active role in information education and as community information experts is a natural outcome of the introduction of new technology into the library. The librarian must move beyond the role of moral guardian and beyond a technical service attitude toward patrons, must make professional judgments regarding the community's information needs, and then must build services and programs to meet those needs.

Service

Can librarians continue to be nonreflective, neutral information brokers providing on-demand service to patrons, more concerned about losing market share and offsetting costs of services than meeting the information needs of the entire community? Can the patrons, many of whom have been trained to think of the library as an "information quick stop," accept the requirement that they take personal responsibility for their information needs and recognize the potential complexity and range of information resources that are available to them and the library?

The proposal to change the library's service orientation to a more educational model has many ramifications for library administration and reference, including the amount of time needed to effectively serve patrons, the issue of librarian neutrality, the usefulness of on-demand reference service, the role of the professional librarian, and the anonymity of the profession.

First let us define the presumptions behind this educational model: (1) information is important; (2) information is not neutral; (3) the librarian's job is to assess the patron's needs and skills and plan a strategy for the patron to access and evaluate needed information; (4) the patron's job is to evaluate the information provided and to use it to meet their needs; (5) the librarian is responsible for providing the best information possible; and finally (6) the patron is required to disclose their information needs in order for the librarian to offer the best assistance.

This model helps to clarify the librarian's role as an information guide able to direct the patron down the most appropriate paths and help them make the best decisions for their individual situation. It also places responsibility on the patron to be an active participant in the information process, not just a passive recipient of decontextualized information. It makes patrons aware that the focus of the library's "moral mission" is the responsible and sophisticated use of information, not the cultivation of particular moral views on other subjects.

The provision of this type of service would entail, in some library settings, a major rethinking of the role of the reference desk, especially the amount of time allocated to reference transactions and the wisdom of the current emphasis on "on demand" reference service. With increasing numbers of requests and decreasing staff it would be a luxury to be able to follow through with each patron and provide more of an educational experience than the present "McDonaldization" of reference service. But if we accept that we have an ethical responsibility to the patron and that a more educational model of reference will best meet the information needs of the community and the individual, then decisions will have to be made about allocation of resources and the need for additional staff.

There is no easy solution to this problem; the realities of a library's fiscal condition cannot be denied. If the library is to position itself as an ethical, concerned player in the information age, then discussions about appropriate levels of patron service will have to take place.

One way of working toward this model has been discussed widely in the academic library literature. Books such as *Rethinking Reference* point out some of the shortcomings of the traditional on-demand reference service in the academic setting.[4] While a number of potential new models of reference have been presented, the concept of "tiered reference" is one that can perhaps be used to manage reference service focused on patron information education.

Tiered reference begins by determining the appropriate level of information needed by a patron and then referring the patron to the appropriate information provider. This type of service assumes that there are various types of questions and that not all require the same level of intervention. For many academic libraries this also places the professional librarian in more of a consultant role, removed from the reference desk and available by appointment or in some cases on demand. The assumption is that for many patrons the information needed goes beyond the answer to a discrete question but will require an in-depth reference interview, analysis of existing sources, and other educational skills.

The tiered reference model also changes the relationship, between the staff and the professionals. For some it gives (the nonprofessionals, staff usually the frontline interviewers) too much autonomy and authority to make decisions regarding the information needs of the patron. For others, it is questionable because it emphasizes the distinction between the staff members and librarians by strictly defining who should answer specific types of questions. The decision to move to an educational model, whether or not tiered reference is used, will change the way that library workers interact with each other and with the public.

Concerns about tiered reference include doubts about the ability of the initial contact person to determine the appropriate level of service for a question, the need to change patrons' perceptions of reference service, and the potential lack of timely answers to information needs. What this model does provide is one way of institutionalizing the relative value that should be given to inquiry and the information needs of the public. The current assumption is that those needs can best be met in a two minute interchange at an overcrowded, noisy reference desk by an overworked, perhaps harried librarian.

The educational model also allows us to again examine the issue of neutrality. If one of our assumptions is the nonneutrality of information, then the librarian is in a position to assist the patron in determining the particular stance or motive of a given publication. The answer to the question, "Which source do you think is better?" can be answered by the professional based on knowledge and experience with information sources. If we are trained to be professional information workers, why should we be unwilling to offer judgments and opinions about the materials we work with every day? This type of service does not imply either the exclusion of materials from the library due to immoral content or the need to evaluate the appropriateness of the information request, but it does imply that the librarian is able to give advice about information sources without the fear that they are violating some ethical standard.

Applying this thinking to the famous Hauptman and Dowd experiments, one would not advocate that librarians initially refuse service to a patron or that they express moral outrage at the request. In the course of a more involved reference interview, however, the librarian could better assess the nature of the patron's interest, propose that other aspects of the topic be considered, and ultimately determine the appropriateness of the library's involvement in the patron's project. Apparently no one advocates that librarians are obligated to help patrons with illegal plans or requests. It follows that if patrons should be obligated to disclose more information about their search needs, reference librarians will be better equipped to determine the legitimacy of their requests. Ultimately, the Hauptman and Dowd cases pose serious dilemmas for librarians already constrained by a strict view of neutrality.

This mode of operation also calls into question another common aspect of reference service, the anonymity of the librarian. Joan Durrance discusses some of the problems of anonymity in her article "The Generic Librarian," presenting the argument that the current ideal in most libraries of reference services provided by anonymous librarians is a deterrent to good service.[5] She gives the various reasons for anonymity and, while acknowledging that there are some valid concerns such as the fear of harassment, argues that there are substantial benefits to abandoning anonymity. According to Durrance, the service provided by the librarian should be compared to service provided by other professionals—teachers, health care workers, accountants, lawyers—where identification is used to establish the rapport needed to fully assist their clients, to be available for follow up information, and to be accountable for the information provided. Therefore, a discussion of anonymity and accountability needs to be considered as an important step in the model proposed.

The educational model of service also demands more from the patron. The move to a purely service driven library has resulted in the patron's expecting to have information provided quickly, efficiently and in most cases with little effort, except maybe to show up, and even that is not required in telephone and online reference service. How will the traditional patron react when faced with the challenge of becoming a more active participant in the search for information? Are libraries willing to take the risk that by demanding more of the patron—more time, more involvement in the process, and more respect for the power of information—the library might be seen as a less "friendly" and "helpful" place?

The desire to make libraries friendly and inviting places may make it difficult for librarians to demand more of their patrons. Librarians have been taught that their job is to ease the burden of the patron, to efficiently provide them with information and to make the library an indispensable part of their lives. But the truth might be that by such efficient delivery of service and by the failure to share the inquiry experience fully with the patron, the patron may believe that reference work, and all library work, is a job that anyone can do, like the clerk at the hardware store who can locate the correct pipe fitting quickly and efficiently. The problem with this way of thinking about the library, of course, is that it misconstrues or ignores the complexity of inquiry and the difficult tasks of information storage and retrieval and the skills needed to use and understand information sources and data.

Not only are these perceptual matters a potential liability for libraries and their continued funding and existence, they also lead to a disservice to the public. If our profession truly believes in the power and importance of information then we should not be encouraging a diminished respect for the process of responsibly providing access to it. This type of attitude will encourage an uncritical approach to the leading information sources of the new technology era. Already, anecdotes abound to suggest that people are too gullible in their evaluation of information on Usenet newsgroups and the World Wide Web.

The educational model also challenges some of the traditional views regarding what details we may request from the patron. If the task is taken seriously of educating the patron about the best possible sources to meet their information needs, the patron needs to be willing to share with the librarian the full scope and range of those needs. An unwillingness to inquire about intent, while perhaps noble in purpose, may mean that librarians are not most effectively meeting their patrons' needs.

If librarians consider themselves to have a professional relationship with their patrons, those patrons need to commit themselves to providing as much information as is needed to make an appropriate diagnosis, to use a medical analogy. With that information, library services can be well planned and more efficient. The need for disclosure of intent by the patron is not in order to judge, criticize, ridicule, or attempt to change the patron's mind. There is still no place for personal judgments about the appropriateness of the request, but there is a need for full disclosure to best meet the patron's needs.

The discussion so far has led to the following conclusions: (1) the size and complexity of today's collections mean that attempts by groups within the community to impose a set of moral values on the library are not feasible;

(2) the community must move away from their view of the library as a moral guardian and (3) that role is to be replaced by the library as an educational force in the community; (4) the library has a professional responsibility to plan how to meet the information needs of the entire community; and (5) the move to education will change the way that the library interacts with patrons. More time and involvement will be required to meet the information needs of the individual.

An obvious response to these statement could be, What if our stakeholders, whoever they might be, do not agree? What if a community is in unanimous accord that the library should be a strong moral agent or that they do not have a need to be active participants in the search for information? Can the library force this model on the public? The answer is no, but the ramifications of letting the public dictate the direction of library service are many. Can libraries, as they have evolved in the United States, go back to the type of institution they were at the turn of the century? Are librarians willing to give up their commitment to intellectual freedom and their status as professional?

Historically, libraries have always been in a state of change, responding to the needs of the culture and to powerful interest groups; those changes have led to the library systems that we currently enjoy and cherish. There is no reason to believe that libraries cannot and will not undergo more radical change in the next hundred years. The direction of that change can be dictated by the outside forces of society, as it was in the past, or it can be shaped and molded by the professionals who have made provision of library service their careers. Either way libraries will not be the same even in the next decade. How librarians make ethical decisions regarding their role in the community and the value of information will have a major impact on the future of libraries and the lives of their patrons.

Chapter 5

Conclusion

Each chapter in this book has approached the problem of information ethics from a distinct perspective or source. We started by trying to think about information itself and its moral value. Then we looked for the source of a new professional ethic for librarians by taking a critical view of the profession's current code of ethics and the organizational structure of libraries. Just as moral theory and theories of information provided a source for thinking about the moral value of information, so organizational theory and thinking about the value of professionalism provided a basis for reflection on how librarians ought to articulate their mission and organize their work. Another crucial part of our study has been an historical review and analysis of key defining issues in the history of public librarianship in this country. Seeing similarities between previous and current issues, and challenging some commonplace assumptions about the way librarians have come to their current understanding of themselves, we positioned ourselves to describe our vision of their future.

In Chapter 4, we made a variety of recommendations for resolving information age library ethics problems. In some cases, these suggestions came directly out of our earlier studies. For example, the "process approach" recommended early in that chapter was influenced by the view of organizational ethics we advocated in Chapter 2. Also, our approach to Internet access was influenced by our reading of the history of the "fiction problem" in Chapter 3. But beyond these discrete connections, we wanted to advocate a more general "ideal" of librarianship.

The immediate and obvious objection to describing an ideal for a profession as diverse as librarianship is that no one description will fit very many librarians. Perhaps our work to this point has already strained the credulity of academic and special librarians who see less of an analogy between their work and public librarianship than we do. Still, a descriptive ideal can be useful if one realizes that "librarianship" is a collaborative effort and, therefore, the ideal of librarianship is a goal realized by groups of professionals. Thus the ideal of librarianship refers more to what the profession aims to achieve as a collective entity than to a composite of virtues that any one person could embody.

The Ideal of the Information Age Librarian

The information age librarian confronts the great changes and coming uncertainties in librarianship by staying focused on the core values that any information technology must serve. Those values are discerned by thinking about the moral value of information in the lives of patrons. The kind of thinking and discussion one needs to engage in to consistently appreciate the moral value of information is not itself technical or technological. It is a qualitative reflection on why sophisticated information skills are important to living well in a technological culture. Thus, underlying our ideal of librarianship in a technological age is a conviction that librarians need to have a candid and ongoing discussion of the humanistic conception of the value of information. This discussion would serve as the background against which choices about technology can be made.

To some, this "values-centered" conception of professional mission will seem like a dangerous departure from the ideal of neutrality embodied in the librarian's commitment to "open access" to information. After all, whose conception of "living well" are librarians to choose? Which "humanistic conception" of information is to be promoted? Does not the librarian's professional credibility depend upon their complete agnosticism with regard to various conceptions of the good life?

Intellectual freedom and a commitment to open inquiry are clearly among the moral constants in librarianship, and so they should remain. But our understanding of these ideals requires rethinking in light of new technology. As we have argued, there has always been a subtle inconsistency in the librarian's advocacy of both neutrality and professional judgment about the quality of materials. Wearing the "neutrality hat," librarians can say that they do not let substantive judgments about content affect their professional agenda. On the other hand, most librarians have acted on a professional judgment about what resources their patrons need. What makes the inconsistency a glaring one is the advent of information technologies such as the Internet which force librarians to articulate their relative loyalties to openness and quality more clearly.

In the information age "open access" becomes inevitable for some resources and, in a technical sense, easy. On the other hand, librarians are right to be uncomfortable when they realize that their commitment to "openness" has allowed a flood of poor quality information into the library. A tension which used to be managed by convenient appeals to "limited resources" in the selection of competing points of view now requires a more absolute choice between "openness" and "quality." The challenge for librarians committed to neutrality and openness is to understand what place, if any, their ability to make judgments about quality has in their professional practice.

Still, the worry that librarians might return to the "bad old days" of voluntary censorship and partisan involvement in public affairs is real. We try to steer a middle path by recommending that librarians drop any pretense of neutrality about the importance of information or their ability to make credible judgements about the integrity and quality of various sources. While the conceptions of the "good life" which librarians implicitly support should be broad and inclusive, librarians should not deny that they are competent to make substantive choices about what resources to value, or that in doing so, they are unapologetically favoring some ways of living over others.

Part of the new landscape of librarianship in the information age is that the relationship between the librarian and the library collection is changing. In a traditional monograph-based collection, the librarian's professional work was directly mirrored in the quality and condition of the physical collection of a specific library. One can imagine the pride in work that might have resulted from years of accumulation, cataloging, and promotion of local resources to patrons. Surely, library users in the past knew that there were far more resources than the local library had, but since that was a given, the focus of the patron's interest was naturally on the physical collection of the local library.

By contrast, the information age library is a point of departure for information and culture which lies beyond its walls. Librarians still take a long range interest in their local collections, but they and their patrons know that the library can do much more. As the ratio between accessible information and holdings grows geometrically, information age librarians naturally focus on guiding their patrons through new oceans of information. The library's "collection" no longer speaks for itself, since the newest additions to the library are as likely to be electronic gateways to other resources as books.

In this environment the ability of librarians to help patrons think critically about their information needs will become if paramount importance. As the librarian's direct control of the "look and feel" of the collection slips away, the importance of the professional expertise of the librarian as an "information consultant" comes to the fore. For example, when a patron of a traditional, early twentieth century library consulted the printed catalog for books and serials on "herb gardening," the librarian might well have known in advance the results of the search. He or she may even have chosen or read the books the patron found. In an information age library, the avenues for exploring the same subject are dizzying. An expert librarian could know only in general terms what kind of information each search avenue might retrieve. What the ideal librarian of today can do better than his or her predecessor, however, is think critically about the "fit" between the information available to the patron and its suitability to their goals.

With the increased use of information technology in libraries, some librarians worry that they are becoming instructional aides in the conduct of computer searches. The ideal we are describing moves librarians in the opposite direction. The greater access to information in today's libraries leaves patrons in greater need of more involved and complex professional consultation in their searches. Information age librarians focus their expertise on helping patrons make prudent decisions about how to evaluate and work with the results of their inquiries, knowing as they do how overwhelming those results can be. We see the impersonal technology of the information age as presenting an opportunity for librarianship to intensify its focus on the personal, professional relationship between librarian and patron.

There are new challenges for the librarian involved with technical service issues as well. How to control and provide access to services and materials that may be available in the library but not owned by the library is a daunting task. The need for new and imaginative ways to catalog and classify materials is a call for librarians to creatively apply those skills to new materials and products. Without meaningful access to the contents of the Internet and other forms of new technology, the technology has no purpose and the library ill serves the patron and the community as a whole.

At the same time, we think librarians should broaden their concept of who the patron is. Traditional librarianship is focused on service to the walk-in patron, even though many libraries have recently experimented with telephone and online reference service. In the course of our argument in this book, we have mentioned the new roles for librarians in assessing their community's use of information and designing programming for the community. To some extent libraries do this already when, for instance, they design special programs to allow day care centers to check out books as corporate clients and even receive visiting "storytellers" from the library staff. Adult literacy programs are another example of a current, systematic response to a community's information needs.

Librarians might go further, however, by promoting sophisticated information skills for corporate and government "patrons." While librarians should continue to target the individual patron and traditionally disadvantaged groups for special services, they should also develop the kind of expertise required to consult with communities that are redesigning their "information infrastructure." Librarians are well situated to be advocates for the public in decisions about how local spending on telecommunications affects the public's access to information. Ten years ago, few people would have thought that the regulation of cable and telephone equipment suppliers had a "library impact," but now we know that it clearly does since libraries plan the cost of expanding their services with an eye to the cost and bandwidth of the community's information infrastructure.

The information age librarian thinks about information as a complex, distributed resource which is not only used by patrons in the satisfaction of their individual interests, but also by groups within the community whose information needs can sometimes be "brokered" by librarians for the public good.

Our ideal librarian is more willing to make judgments about the quality of different resources, more involved in their patrons' needs through tiered reference and reference consulting, and more active in community affairs which affect the public's access to information. Beyond this, librarians can become the "public intellectuals" of the information age by developing expertise and public programming on issues of immediate concern to their communities. Some libraries already do this through workshops, seminars, and sponsorship of reading groups, but in most libraries these programs are the first to be sacrificed to budget cuts.

In public libraries, this role could be expanded by increasing coverage of community affairs on important community issues such as crime, economic development, and transportation. In academic libraries, library faculty could become "interdisciplinary role models" by working with teaching and research faculty to broaden their discipline centered approaches to topics. Not every community needs such programming and not every faculty member needs to have their research focus broadened, but one of the distinctive contributions of the sophisticated present-day librarian is precisely the ability to bring together diverse kinds of information and make critical judgments about their quality. The information age librarian may be less of a "collector" than his or her historical counterpart and more of a "selector" and "presenter."

Our ideal librarian is involved with a broader range of patrons in more complex professional relationships. The "clients" of the information age librarian are interested not only in the library's holdings but in the librarian's professional expertise. Instead of thinking about the information resources of the library as the library's "capital," the library system should place a new emphasis on the "human capital" of the librarian's expertise as a resource worthy of investment. We advocate broadening the range of professional development opportunities for librarians so that they can acquire and improve their subject specific knowledge, presentation skills, and technical skills to keep pace with technology and the new demands of their mission. By investing in new areas of specialization such as information systems, community affairs, business information services, or public policy, libraries can offer more sophisticated consulting and educational services to the community.

The ideal we are describing will require both the reallocation of resources and new financial commitments from library sponsors. In academic settings, it will require a strong commitment to the "faculty" status of the librarian, which often brings with it greater independence in the planning of research programs and teaching initiatives.

Finally, the workplace of the librarian who is to realize the ideal we propose will support self-governance, collaboration, and professional development. It will be a place where professional colleagues meet as peers to set priorities and hold each other accountable to meeting them. In pursuing a values-centered mission, librarians will have to engage more frequently in value-rich discussion about their experiences with patrons. As the information age librarians develop more public education programs, they will need more independence and authority to plan and implement programs.

But even in the brave new world of the information age, where librarians can meet as peers in organizations that support their professional growth and work with their communities to meet the information needs of the library stakeholders, there will be no set answers to the ethical problems that they will continue to face, the old ones that echo from the past and the new ones that have yet to be heard. The answers to many of those problems will still need to be addressed in a matter of moments during days short on time and long on assignments. The most that the librarian can hope for is that prior to that point there has been reflection, discussion and the development of organizational and personal values that can be called upon to deal with specific situations. The time for complacency and benign neglect regarding our professional morals and ethics has passed. New discussions and dialogues will shape the future.

Appendix: American Library Association

The following codes of ethics are reprinted with the permission of the American Library Association

The 1939 Code of Ethics for Librarians

Preamble

1. The library as an institution exists for the benefit of a given constituency, whether it be citizens of a community, members of an educational institution, or some larger or more specialized group. Those who enter the library profession assume an obligation to maintain ethical standards of behavior in relation to the governing authority under which they work, to the library constituency, to the library as an institution and to fellow workers on the staff, to other members of the library profession, and to society in general.

2. The term librarian in this code applies to any person who is employed by a library to do work that is recognized to be professional in character according to standards established by the American Library Association.

3. This code sets forth principles of ethical behavior for the professional librarian. It is not a declaration of prerogatives nor a statement of recommended practices in specific situations.

I. Relation of the librarian to the governing authority

4. The librarian should perform his duties with realization of the fact that final jurisdiction over the administration of the library rests in the officially constituted governing authority. This authority may be vested in a designated individual, or in a group such as a committee or board.

5. The chief librarian should keep the governing authority informed on professional standards and progressive action. Each librarian should be responsible for carrying out the policies of the governing authority and its appointed executives with a spirit of loyalty to the library.

6.   The chief librarian should interpret decisions of the governing authority to the staff, and should act as liaison officer in maintaining friendly relations between staff members and those in authority.

7.   Recommendations to the governing authority for the appointment of a staff member should be made by the chief librarian solely upon the basis of the candidate's professional and personal qualifications for the position. Continuance in service and promotion should depend upon the quality of performance, following a definite and known policy. Whenever the good of the service requires a change in personnel, timely warning should be given. If desirable adjustment cannot be made, unsatisfactory service should be terminated in accordance with the policy of the library and the rules of tenure.

8.   Resolutions, petitions, and requests of a staff organization or group should be submitted through a duly appointed representative to the chief librarian. If a mutually satisfactory solution cannot be reached, the chief librarian, on request of the staff, should transmit the matter to the governing authority. The staff may further request that they be allowed to send a representative to the governing authority, in order to present their opinions.

II. Relation of the librarian to his constituency

9.   The chief librarian, aided by staff members in touch with the constituency, should study the present and future needs of the library, and should acquire materials on the basis of those needs. Provision should be made for as wide a range of publications and as varied a representation of viewpoints as is consistent with the policies of the library and with the funds available.

10.   It is the librarian's responsibility to make the resources and services of the library known to its potential users. Impartial service should be rendered to all who are entitled to use the library.

11.   It is the librarian's obligation to treat as confidential any private information obtained through contact with library patrons.

12.   The librarian should try to protect library property and to inculcate in users a sense of their responsibility for its preservation.

III. Relations of the librarian within his library

13.   The chief librarian should delegate authority, encourage a sense of responsibility and initiative on the part of staff members, provide for their professional development, and appreciate good work. Staff members should be informed of the duties of their positions and the policies and problems of the library.

14.   Loyalty to fellow workers and a spirit of courteous cooperation, whether between individuals or between departments, are essential to effective library service.

15.   Criticism of library policies, service, and personnel should be offered only to the proper authority for the sole purpose of improvement of the library.

16.   Acceptance of a position in a library incurs an obligation to remain long enough to repay the library for the expenses incident to adjustment. A contract signed or agreement made should be adhered to faithfully until it expires or is dissolved by mutual consent.

17.   Resignations should be made long enough before they are to take effect to allow adequate time for the work to be put in shape and a successor appointed.

18.   A librarian should never enter into a business dealing on behalf of the library which will result in personal profit.

19.   A librarian should never turn the library's resources to personal use, to the detriment of services which the library renders to its patrons.

IV. Relation of the librarian to his profession

20.   Librarians should recognize librarianship as an educational profession and realize that the growing effectiveness of their service is dependent upon their own development.

21.   In view of the importance of ability and personality traits in library work, a librarian should encourage only those persons with suitable aptitudes to enter the library profession and should discourage the continuance in service of the unfit.

22.   Recommendations should be confidential and should be fair to the candidate and the prospective employer by presenting an unbiased statement of strong and weak points.

23.   Librarians should have a sincere belief and a critical interest in the library profession. They should endeavor to achieve and maintain adequate salaries and proper working conditions.

24.   Formal appraisal of the policies or practices of another library should be given only upon the invitation of that library's governing authority or chief librarian.

25.   Librarians, in recognizing the essential unity of their profession, should have membership in library organizations and should be ready to attend and participate in library meetings and conferences.

V. Relation of the librarian to society

26.   Librarians should encourage a general realization of the value of library service and be informed concerning movements, organizations, and institutions whose aims are compatible with those of the library.

27.   Librarians should participate in public and community affairs and so represent the library that it will take its place among educational, social, and cultural agencies.

28.   A librarian's conduct should be such as to maintain public esteem for the library and for library work.

Statement on Professional Ethics, 1975

Introduction

The American Library Association has a special concern for the free flow of information and ideas. Its views have been set forth in such policy statements as the Library Bill of Rights and the Freedom to Read Statement where it has said clearly that in addition to the generally accepted legal and ethical principles and the respect for intellectual freedom which should guide the action of every citizen, membership in the library profession carries with it special obligations and responsibilities.

Every citizen has the right as an individual to take part in public debate or to engage in social and political activity.

The only restrictions on these activities are those imposed by specific and well-publicized laws and regulations which are generally applicable. However, since personal views and activities may be interpreted as representative of the institution in which a librarian is employed, proper precaution should be taken to distinguish between private actions and those one is authorized to take in the name of an institution. The statement which follows sets forth certain ethical norms which, while not exclusive to, are basic to librarianship. It will be augmented by explanatory interpretations and additional statements as they may be needed.

The Statement

A Librarian

Has a special responsibility to maintain the principles of the *Library Bill of Rights*.

Should learn and faithfully execute the policies of the institution of which one is a part and should endeavor to change those which conflict with the spirit of the *Library Bill of Rights*.

Must protect the essential confidential relationship which exists between a library user and the library.

Must avoid any possibility of personal financial gain at the expense of the employing institution.

Has an obligation to insure equality of opportunity and fair judgement of competence in actions dealing with staff appointments, retentions, and promotions.

Has an obligation when making appraisals of the qualifications of any individual to report the facts clearly, accurately, and without prejudice, according to generally accepted guidelines concerning the disclosing of personal information.

Statement on Professional Ethics, 1981

Introduction

Since 1939, the American Library Association has recognized the importance of codifying and making known to the public and the profession the principles which guide librarians in action. This latest revision of the Code of Ethics reflects changes in the nature of the profession and in its social and institutional environment. It should be revised and augmented as necessary.

Librarians significantly influence or control the selection, organization, preservation, and dissemination of information. In a political system grounded in an informed citizenry, librarians are members of a profession explicitly committed to intellectual freedom and the freedom of access to information. We have a special obligation to ensure the free flow of information and ideas to present and future generations.

Librarians are dependent upon one another for the bibliographical resources that enable us to provide information services, and have obligations for maintaining the highest level of personal integrity and competence.

Code of Ethics

I.   Librarians must provide the highest level of service through appropriate and usefully organized collections, fair and equitable circulation and service policies, and skillful, accurate, unbiased, and courteous responses to all requests for assistance.

II.   Librarians must resist all efforts by groups or individuals to censor library materials.

III.   Librarians must protect each user's right to privacy with respect to information sought or received, and materials consulted, borrowed, or acquired.

IV.   Librarians must adhere to the principles of due process and equality of opportunity in peer relationships and personnel actions.

V.   Librarians must distinguish clearly in their actions and statements between their personal philosophies and attitudes and those of an institution or professional body.

VI.   Librarians must avoid situations in which personal interests might be served or financial benefits gained at the expense of library users, colleagues, or the employing institution.

The 1995 Code of Ethics

As members of the American Library Association, we recognize the importance of codifying and making known to the profession and to the general public the ethical principles that guide the work of librarians, other professionals providing information services, library trustees and library staffs.

Ethical dilemmas occur when values are in conflict. The American Library Association Code of Ethics states the values to which we are committed, and embodies the ethical responsibilities of the profession in this changing information environment.

We significantly influence or control the selection, organization, preservation, and dissemination of information. In a political system grounded in an informed citizenry, we are members of a profession explicitly committed to intellectual freedom and the freedom of access to information. We have a special obligation to ensure the free flow of information and ideas to present and future generations.

The principles of this Code are expressed in broad statements to guide ethical decision making. These statements provide a framework; they cannot and do not dictate conduct to cover particular situations.

I.   We provide the highest level of service to all library users through appropriate and usefully organized resources; equitable service policies; equitable access; and accurate, unbiased, and courteous responses to all requests.

II.   We uphold the principles of intellectual freedom and resist all efforts to censor library resources.

III.   We protect each library user's right to privacy and confidentiality with respect to information sought or received and resources consulted, borrowed, acquired or transmitted.

IV.   We recognize and respect intellectual property rights.

V.   We treat co-workers and other colleagues with respect, fairness and good aith, and advocate conditions of employment that safeguard the rights and welfare of all employees of our institutions.

VI.   We do not advance private interests at the expense of library users, colleagues, or our employing institutions.

VII.   We distinguish between our personal convictions and professional duties and do not allow our personal beliefs to interfere with fair representations of the aims of our institutions or the provision of access to their information resources.

VIII.   We strive for excellence in the profession by maintaining and enhancing our own knowledge and skills, by encouraging the professional development of coworkers, and by fostering the aspirations of potential members of the profession.

Chapter Notes

Introduction

1.   Robert Hauptman, "Professionalism or Culpability? An Experiment in Ethics," *Wilson Library Bulletin* 50 (April 1976) 626–627. In a variation on Hauptman's experiment, Robert Dowd visited thirteen libraries dressed in the garb of a drug user and asked for reference help to learn how to freebase cocaine. While only four of the libraries had the information requested, none refused to help him on ethical grounds; see also: R.C. Dowd, "I Want to Find Out How to Freebase Cocaine: Or, Yet Another Unobtrusive Test of Reference Performance," *Reference Librarian* 25–26 (1989) 483–493.

2.   Samuel S. Green, "Personal Relations between Librarians and Readers," *American Library Journal* 1 (October 1976) 74–81.

3.   On the other hand, there is good reason to think that early library leaders such as Melvil Dewey did experience conflicts of interest. For more information, see Dee Garrison, *Apostles of Culture: The Public Librarian and American Society, 1876–1920* (New York: Free Press, 1979) 105–166.

4.   Norman D. Stevens, "Ethical Considerations in Representation, or, Did Dui Do It?" *Library Trends* 40 (Fall 1991) 303–320.

5.   D. J. Foskett, *The Creed of a Librarian: No Politics, No Religion, No Morals* (London: Library Association, 1962; reprint, London: Library Association, 1970) reprint 10.

6.   See the Appendix, page 155.

7.   Gillian S. Gremmels, "Reference in the Public Interest: An Examination of Ethics," *RQ* 30 (Fall 1990) 362–369.

8.   *Ibid.*, 368.

9.   *Ibid.*, 364–365.

10.   T. J. Froehlich, "Ethics, Ideologies, and Practices of Information Technology and Systems," *ASIS '90: Proceedings of the 53rd Meeting of ASIS* (Medford, N.J.: Learned Information, 1990).

11.   For example, to solve public health problems we created new obligations for doctors to report disease and abuse. To prevent fraud and deception in the financial services industry, financial advisors took on new obligations to disclose information to clients.

12.   Indeed, the opposing argument to this is fallacious. Most practitioners of most professions are never in a position to significantly affect the object of their profession, yet the collective effect of their labors is to produce, and reproduce, that object. For example, only a few scientists are in a position to steer research in their field toward or away from specific goals or topics, yet the whole profession is involved in the validation and furtherance of those research agendas.

13.   For a comprehensive collection of documents relating to such controversy and the broader "Cyberporn Debate," see URL: http://www2000.ogsm.vanderbilt.edu/cyberporn.debate.cgi. This site, maintained by *Project 2000*, "Research Program on Marketing in Computer-Mediated Environments," Donna L. Hoffman and Thomas P. Novack, Vanderbilt University, includes a collection of links about the apparent lapse in review procedures by the *Georgetown Law Journal*, in its unusual prepublication arrangement with the author of a research article claiming that a very high percentage of Internet users are accessing pornography through newsgroups. Serious doubts about the integrity of the study have been raised, leading some to wonder about the adequacy of the journal's review process.

14.   C. Osburn, "The Structuring of the Scholarly Communication System," *College and Research Libraries* 50 (1989) 272–287, quoted in Gordon Moran and Michael Mallory, "Some Ethical Considerations Regarding Scholarly Communications," *Library Trends* 40 (Fall 1991) 351.

15.   H. Schneider, "The Threat to Authority in the Revolution of Chemistry," *History of Universities* 8 (1989) 137–150, quoted in Moran and Michael Mallory, "Some Ethical Considerations."

16.   Broadly conceived to include knowledge and cultural production. In Chapter 1, a more rigorous definition of the term, is undertaken.

17.   Daniel C. Dennett, "Information, Technology, and the Virtues of Ignorance," *Daedalus* 115 (Summer 1986) 135–153, and Mark Alfino, "Do Expert Systems have a Moral Cost?" *Journal of Information Ethics* 2:2 (Fall 1993) 15–19.

18.   Patrick Williams, *The American Public Library and the Problem of Purpose* (New York: Greenwood Press, 1988) 41–63.

19.   *Ibid.*

Chapter 1

1.   In late antiquity, Stoics argued that philosophers (literally, "lovers of wisdom") can face adversity better. Early in the Christian era, "Lady Philosophy" appeared to Boethius in his jail cell to explain why it is better to have knowledge even if it gets you in trouble. By the 17th and 18th centuries, Enlightenment thinkers as diverse as Bacon and Condorcet expressed their optimism that the progress of knowledge would improve the material and moral condition of man.

2.   What puzzles some people about these shifts in usage is that we are still wedded to the idea that information transfer is something that requires an intentional human mind. But the cybernetic and scientific usages of the terms demonstrate the expendability of that assumption. For a highly theoretical treatment of this trend in the fields of knowledge see François Lyotard, *The Postmodern Condition* (Minneapolis: University of Minnesota Press, 1984).

3.   Theodore Roszak, *The Cult of Information* (Berkeley University of California Press, 1994). In this remarkable polemic, Roszack argues, for instance, that "ideas," which are the source of knowledge, contain no information.

4.   Many writers in diverse disciplines have called attention to this demographic shift, which is variously referred to as the emergence of the "knowledge worker," "information worker," or "symbolic analyst."

5.   The relationship between speech and writing in the Western philosophical tradition has been the object of vigorous study since the publication of work by Jacques Derrida, including, for instance, his *Grammatology* (Baltimore: Johns Hopkins University Press,

1974). More traditional scholarship has focused on several key texts in Plato, including the *Phaedrus* and the *Seventh Letter*.

6. Robert Lucky, *Silicon Dreams* (New York: St. Martin's, 1963) 20.

7. Philosophically speaking, there may be no such thing as raw data, since even the simplest measure of a phenomenon is informed by a process of selection and a distinction of each datum from other possible readings.

8. Roszak argues, to the contrary, that "great ideas" such as the idea of political equality contain no information. See Theodore Roszak, *The Cult of Information*, produced by Arthur Bloch, 30 minutes, Thinking Allowed Productions, 1988, videocassette.

9. Later, we will consider a challenge to the assumption that knowledge is intrinsically valuable. In the present argument we are relying on a common sense intuition, also defended by philosophers, that a life pursuing knowledge is always preferable.

10. Most people forget that so called "Miranda rights" are only as old as the 1966 ruling: *Miranda v. Arizona*, 384 U.S. 426 (1966). Remembering this helps us keep in mind the historical development at work in our understanding of rights.

11. In the strict legal sense, there is no fundamental "right to education" (only a right to equal treatment in the state's efforts to educate citizens), but morally most people would now think it unconscionable to allow someone to go without educational services.

12. John Rawls, *A Theory of Justice* (Cambridge, Mass.: Harvard University Press, 1971) 60.

13. *Ibid.*, 101.

14. Pete Giacoma, *The Fee or Free Decision: Legal, Economic, Political, and Ethical Perspectives for Public Libraries* (New York: Neal-Schuman, 1989) 131.

15. Rawls, *A Theory of Justice* 440.

16. Giacoma, *Fee or Free* 132.

17. John Stuart Mill, *Utilitarianism* (Indianapolis: Hackett, 1979) 62.

18. *Ibid.*, 10.

19. Since Gilligan's initial work and later revisions, debate has raged over the causes, validity, and implications of her findings. Some commentators, such as Claudia Card and Catherine MacKinnon, suggest that an "ethics of care" is a product of the subjugation of women and may express women's lack of power rather than an "authentic" moral voice. For more about these and other issues, see Claudia Card, ed., *Feminist Ethics* (Lawrence: University of Kansas Press, 1991).

20. For a discussion of this issue, see Deborah Tannen, *Talking 9 to 5: How Women's and Men's Conversational Styles Affect Who Gets Heard, Who Gets Credit, and What Gets Done at Work* (New York: William Morrow, 1994) or Don Sager, "Do Women and Men Manage Libraries Differently?" *Public Libraries* 34 (May/June 1995) 132–142.

21. For discussion of bias in cataloguing and classification systems, see Sanford Berman, "DDC 19: An Indictment," chapter in *The Joy of Cataloguing: Essays, Letters, Reviews and other Explosions* (Phoenix, AZ: Oryx Press, 1981) 177–185.

22. While this is the main contrast he draws, he also considers two other categories: drudgery and spontaneous interpersonal relations. Jon Elster, "Self-Realization," *Social and Personal Ethics,* ed. William H. Shaw (Belmont, Calif.: Wadsworth, 1993) 204–212.

23. The field of knowledge in which this change is most apparent is logic. The growth of informal logic, which considers the quality of information as integral to the assessment of abstract reasoning, suggests that the traditional isolation of reason is a bias. In the behavioral sciences, new work in "emotional intelligence"—Antonio Damasio, *Descartes' Error: Emotion, Reason, and the Human Brain* (New York: G.P. Putnam's, 1994), and Daniel Goleman, *Emotional Intelligence* (New York: Bantam Books, 1995)—and new ways of thinking about the integration of the brain and the nervous system are leading us to think about reasoning as less isolated from its "data" and much more a natural product of interaction with the environment.

Chapter 2

1. As a foundational issue in the field, this claim is subject to a tremendous amount of interpretive and empirical study. Interpretive models of immoral conduct in an organizational setting often try to show how features of the organizational culture affect moral decision making. See, for instance, L. K. Revino, "Ethical Decision Making in Organizations: A Person-Situation Interactionist Model," *Academy of Management Review* 11 (1986) 601–617. Empirical studies of organizational misconduct try to measure the frequency of various kinds of misconduct and the kind of moral awareness individuals have of their conduct. For a good introduction to these findings and to organizational ethics in general, see Ronald Sims, *Ethics and Organizational Decision Making: A Call for Renewal* (Westport, Conn.: Quorum Books, 1994).

2. See Chapter 1, page 33, for a primer on ethical theory.

3. See, for instance, the debate between Marshall Sashkin and Edwin Locke: Marshall Sashkin, "Participative Management Is an Ethical Imperative," *Organizational Dynamics* 12 (Spring 1984) 4–22; Edwin Locke, David Latham, and Gary Schwiger, "Participation in Decision Making: When Should It Be Used?" *Organizational Dynamics* 14 (Winter 1986) 65–78, Marshall Sashkin, "Participative Management Remains an Ethical Imperative," *Organizational Dynamics* 14 (Spring 1986) 62–74.

4. Jay Galbraith, *Organization Design* (Reading, Mass.: Addison-Wesley, 1977) 11–32.

5. *Ibid.*, 23.

6. Robert Solomon, "Macho Myths and Metaphors," chapter in *Ethics and Excellence* (Oxford: Oxford University Press, 1992) 22–33.

7. William Evan and Edward R. Freeman, "A Stakeholder Theory of the Modern Corporation: Kantian Capitalism," in *Ethical Theory and Business,* ed. Tom Beauchamp and Norman Bowie (Englewood Cliffs, N.J.: Prentice-Hall, 1993) 75–84.

8. It may help to document several prominent examples of research which connects structural organizational theory and ethics. For a structural theory of organizations based on a theory of power and conflict, see Jerald Hage, *Theories of Organizations: Form, Process, and Transformation* (New York: Wiley, 1980). For a more pointed discussion of alienation in work, see Howard Schwartz, "On the Psychodynamics of Organizational Totalitarianism," in *The Psychodynamics of Organizations,* ed. Larry Hirshorn and Carole K. Barnett (Philadelphia: Temple University Press, 1993) 237–250. Recent work in business ethics has specifically tried to analyze organizational structure in terms of its moral harms, drawing on the broader social psychology literature. See, for example, Dennis J. Moberg, "An Ethical Analysis of Hierarchical Relations in Organizations," *Business Ethics Quarterly* 4:2 (April 1994) 205–220.

9. Philip H. Ennis, "Seven Questions about the Profession of Librarianship: An Introduction," *Library Quarterly* 31 (October 1961) 299.

10. Digby Hartridge, "Professional Attitudes and Education for Public Librarianship," in *Education and Training of Information Professionals: Comparative International Perspectives,* ed. G. E. Gorman (Metuchen, N.J.: Scarecrow Press, 1990) 247–260.

11. Diana Woodward, "Teaching Ethics for Information Professionals," *Journal of Education for Library and Information Science* 30 (Fall 1989) 132–135.

12. Michael H. Harris, "Portrait in Paradox: Commitment and Ambivalence in American Librarianship, 1876–1976," *Libri* 26 (1976) 281–301.

13. *Ibid.*, 293.

14. William Birdsall, "Librarianship, Professionalism, and Social Change," *Library Journal* 107 (February 1, 1982) 224, 226.

15. *Ibid.*, 226. For a more extensive treatment of this argument, see William Birdsall, "Librarians and Professionalism, Status Measured by Outmoded Models," *Canadian Library Journal* (June 1980) 145–48.

16. Frederick Frankena and Joann Koelln Frankena, "The Politics of Expertise and Role of the Librarian," *Behavioral and Social Science Librarian* 6 (Fall/Winter 1986) 37.

17. *Ibid.*, 45.

18. *Ibid.*, 44.

19. For example, if we should hear that librarians are in favor of fair housing laws for black or gay Americans, we would not assume that their librarianship led them to this view, but rather that this was the considered view of a professional group with more than average education.

20. For examples, see Rena Corlin, *Codes of Professional Responsibility* (Washington, D.C.: Bureau of National Affairs, 1986).

21. Samuel Rothstein, "In Search of Ourselves," *Library Journal* 93 (January 15, 1968) 156.

22. This was first expressed in the minutes of the ALA Committee on Professional Ethics at their 1992 annual Conference—American Library Association. Committee on Professional Ethics, *Minutes of the 1992 Annual Conference*, San Francisco, California (June 28, 1992) 5. At that time the ALA was encouraging libraries to adopt the ALA Code of Ethics as a matter of institutional commitment. (See American Library Association Public Information Office, "More Than 50 Academic Libraries Adopt ALA Codes of Ethics," June 1992 press release.) The Committee subsequently considered making the code a "pledge" (using "I" as the subject of each item), but decided instead to make it a collective statement. The word "librarians" is replaced by "we" in the transition from the February 1994 draft to the June 1994 draft.

23. Rothstein, "In Search of Ourselves," 157. His list includes: (1) develop collections; (2) arrange and describe these collections for effective use by a broad public; (3) find specific information quickly; (4) advise people on the choice of books; (5) in specific fields, act as a "literature specialist" (compiling bibliographies, abstracting, making reviews of literature); (6) operate libraries.

24. L. Finks, "Librarianship Needs a New Code of Professional Ethics," *American Libraries* 22 (January 1991) 84–88.

25. Russell Bowden, "Professional Responsibilities of Librarians and Information Workers," *IFLA Journal* 20 (1994) 120–129.

26. *Ibid.*, 125.

27. D. H. Borchardt, "Prolegomena to an Austrialian Code of Professional Ethics for Librarians," *Australian Academic and Research Libraries: AARL* 12 (December 1981) 249.

28. Henry Mintzberg, *The Structuring of Organizations: A Synthesis of Research* (Englewood Cliffs, N.J.: Prentice-Hall, 1979) 371.

29. T. D. Webb, *Public Library Organization and Structure* (Jefferson, N.C.: McFarland, 1989).

30. Michael Gorman, "Organization of Academic Libraries in Light of Automation," *Advances in Library Automation and Networking* (Greenwich, Conn.: JAI Press, 1987) 164.

31. For another example of an institution moving away from the technical/public services distinction, see Ross Stephen and John Buschman, "'Compleat' Library Organization: A Case Study of the Academic Library," *Library Administration and Management* 7 (Spring 1993) 79–88.

32. See Sashkin, "Participative Management Is an Ethical Imperative"; Locke, "Participation in Decision Making: When Should It Be Used?" and Sashkin, "Participative Management Remains an Ethical Imperative."

33. Robert Levering, *A Great Place to Work* (New York: Random House, 1988).

34. A. P. N. Thapisa, "Triple-Tier Organizational Structure: Improving the Quality of Work Life through Job Redesign," *British Journal of Academic Librarianship* 5 (1990) 95–117.

35. Still, "devolving" power to teams has its own risks and complications. Margo Crist reports the results of a study of six libraries in which significant reorganization had taken place. See Margo Crist, "Structuring the Academic Library Organization of the Future: Some New Paradigms," *Journal of Library Administration*, 20:2 (1994) 47–65.

36. Ralph G. Lewis and Douglas Smith, "Why Total Quality?" Chapter in *Total Quality in Higher Education* (Delray Beach, Fla.: St. Lucie Press, 1994) 1–19.

37. The problem of benchmarking professional services (as opposed to manufacturing, for instance) is well known in the literature. Professionals often argue that qualitative differences between apparently similar services (such as, for example, two summer reading programs in a public library) making it impossible to benchmark professional services. But there are ways of accounting for qualitative differences without abandoning benchmarking wholesale. For applications of benchmarking to library service, see Alan Powell, "Management Models and Measurement in the Virtual Library," *Special Libraries* 85 (Fall 1994) 260–263.

38. Joanne R. Euster and Peter Haikalis, "Matrix Model of Organization for a University Library Public Services Division," in *Academic Libraries: Myths and Realities: Proceedings of the Third National Conference of the Association of College and Research Libraries*, ed. Suzanne C. Dodson, (Chicago: Association of College and Research Libraries, 1984) 359.

39. It may help to provide examples of each characteristic mentioned above. In work environments with rapid technological change, it is hard to expect a single supervisor to be able to evaluate new and emerging technologies for a work group. Professional librarianship, as we have been describing it, requires autonomy for librarians to make professional judgments about, say, collection development or new, creative patron services, but it also requires coordination with other staff and resources to carry out such projects. This contrasts, for instance, with more individualistic kinds of professional activity, such as humanities research, or professions with individualized professional-client relationships. Finally, matrix organization works well in holistic work settings because it reduces the isolation and segregation engendered by a divisional structure.

40. Martha Montague Smith, "Infoethics for Leaders: Models of Moral Agency in the Information Environment," *Library Trends* 40 (Winter 1992) 553–570.

Chapter 3

1. Michael H. Harris and Stanley Hannah, "Why Do We Study the History of Libraries? A Meditation on the Perils of Ahistoricism in the Information Era," *Library and Information Science Research* 14 (June 1992) 123–130.

2. U.S. Bureau of the Census. *Historical Statistics of the United States, Colonial Times to 1970*, part 2, Bicentennial edition (Washington, D.C.: U.S. Government Printing Office, 1975) 808.

3. *Ibid.*, 810.

4. Josiah Phillips Quincy, "The Function of a Town Library," in *Library and Society*, ed. Arthur E. Bostwick (New York: H.W. Wilson, 1921; reprint, Freeport, N.Y.: Books for Libraries Press, 1968) reprint 56.

5. Patrick Williams, *American Public Library and the Problem of Purpose* (New York: Greenwood Press, 1988) 56.

6. Sidney Ditzion, *Arsenals of a Democratic Culture: A Social History of the American Public Library Movement in New England and the Middle States from 1850 to 1900* (Chicago: American Library Association, 1947) 159.

7. Michael H. Harris, *The Purpose of the American Public Library in Historical Perspective: A Revisionist Interpretation* (ERIC Document 071668, 1972) 19.

8. Moses Coit Tyler, "Historical Evolution of the Free Public Library in America and Its True Function in the Community," in *Library and Society*, ed. Arthur E. Bostwick (New York: H.W. Wilson 1921; reprint, Freeport, N.Y.: Books for Libraries Press, 1968) reprint 23.

9. Michael H. Harris, "The Purpose of the American Public Library: A Revisionist Interpretation of History," *Library Journal* 98 (September 15, 1973) 2510.

10. Dee Garrison, *Apostles of Culture: The Public Librarian and American Society, 1876–1920* (New York: Free Press, 1979) 36.

11. *Ibid.*, 258

12. Hugo Munsterberg, "The Public Library in American Life," in *Library and Society*, ed. Arthur E. Bostwick (New York: H.W. Wilson, 1921; reprint, Freeport, N.Y.: Books for Libraries Press, 1968) reprint 84.

13. Margery Closey Quigley, "Where Neighbors Meet," in *Library and Society*, ed. Arthur E. Bostwick (New York: H.W. Wilson, 1921; reprint, Freeport, N.Y.: Books for Libraries Press, 1968) reprint 443–451.

14. David William Davies, *Public Libraries as Cultural and Social Centers: The Origin of the Concept* (Metuchen, N.J.: Scarecrow Press, 1974).

15. Williams, *American Public Library* 9–24.

16. Garrison, *Apostles of Culture* 71.

17. W.M. Stevenson, "Weeding Out Fiction in the Carnegie Free Library of Allegheny, PA," *Library Journal* 115:11 (June 15, 1990) 72–75.

18. John Berry, "Leaning Toward 'Quality'," *Library Journal,* 115 (June 15, 1990) 71.

19. Nora Rawlinson, "Give 'Em What They Want," *Library Journal* 115:11 (June 15, 1990) 77–79.

20. Esther Jane Carrier, *Fiction in Public Libraries, 1900–1950* (Littleton, Colo: Libraries Unlimited, 1985).

21. Ditzion, *Arsenals of a Democratic Culture* 180.

22. Isabel Ely Lord, "Open Shelves and the Loss of Books," in *The Library Without Walls: Reprints of Papers and Addresses*, ed. Laura M. Janzow (New York: H.W. Wilson, 1927) 191–220.

23. Erastus S. Willcox, "Open Shelves," in *The Library Without Walls: Reprints of Papers and Addresses*, ed. Laura M. Janzow (New York: H.W. Wilson, 1927) 222–236.

24. Samuel Rothstein, "Development of Reference Services Through Academic Traditions, Public Library Practice, and Special Librarianship," *Reference Librarian* 25–26 (1989) 72.

25. William B. Child, "Reference Work at the Columbia College Library," *Library Journal* 16 (October 1891) 298

26. *Ibid.*

27. Garrison, *Apostles of Culture* 208.

28. Samuel S. Green, "Personal Relations Between Librarians and Readers," *American Library Journal* 1 (October 1876) 74–81.

29. Rothstein, "Development of Reference Services" 72.

30. Wendell G. Johnson, "Need for Value Based Reference Policy: John Rawls at the Reference Desk," *Reference Librarian* 47 (1994) 204.

31. Michael McCoy, "Bibliographic Overview: The Ethics of Reference Service," *Reference Librarian* 4 (Summer 1982) 157–162.

32. Robert Hauptman, "Professionalism or Culpability? An Experiment in Ethics," *Wilson Library Bulletin* 50 (April 1976) 626–627.

33. Paul B. Weiner, "Mad Bombers and Ethical Librarians: A Dialogue with Robert Hauptman and John Swan," *Catholic Library World* 58 (January/February 1987) 161–163.

34. Green, *Personal Relations Between Librarians and Readers* 86.

35. R.C. Dowd, "I Want to Find Out How to Freebase Cocaine: Or, Yet Another Unobtrusive Test of Reference Performance," *Reference Librarian* 25–26 (1989) 483–493.

36. Rothstein "Development of Reference Services" 135–155.

37. Samuel Rothstein, "Where Does It Hurt? Identifying the Real Concerns in the Ethics of Reference Service" *Reference Librarian* 4 (Summer 1982) 1–12.

38. Gregory E. Koster, "Ethics in Reference Service: Codes, Case Studies, or Values?" *Reference Services Review* 20 (1992) 77.

39. Wendell G. Johnson, "The Need for Value Based Reference Policy: John Rawls at the Reference Desk," *Reference Librarian* 47 (1994) 207.

40. American Library Association Office for Intellectual Freedom. *Intellectual Freedom Manual*, 4th ed. (Chicago: American Library Association, 1992) xiii.

41. George Franklin Bowerman, *Censorship and the Public Library with Other Papers* (Freeport, N.Y.: Books for Libraries Press, 1931) 65.

42. "Questions and Answers about *American Psycho*," *Publishers Weekly* (March 15, 1991) 9.

43. Amy Heilsberg, "Self-Censorship Starts Early: A Library School Student Learns an Unexpected Lesson When She Takes on a Touchy Topic," *American Libraries* 25 (September 1994) 768.

44. Evelyn Geller, "Intellectual Freedom: Eternal Principle or Unanticipated Consequence?" *Library Journal* 99 (May 15, 1974) 1364–1367.

45. Geller, *Intellectual Freedom* 1366.

46. Harris, "The Purpose of the American Public Library," (1973).

47. Dorothy Broderick, "Censorship Reevaluated," *Library Journal*, 96 (November 15, 1971) 3816-1818.

48. Harris, "Purpose of the American Public Library," (1973) 2514.

49. Robert Boguslaw's comments concerning the responsibilities of human beings in the age of cyberculture are paraphrased in Nolan E. Shepard, "Technology: Messiah or Monster?" in *Monster or Messiah? The Computer's Impact on Society*, ed. Walter M. Matthews (Jackson: University of Mississippi, 1990) 153.

50. John Swan, "Lies, Damned Lies, and Democracy *and* The Ethics of Freedom," in *The Freedom to Lie: A Debate About Democracy*, John Swan and Noel Peattie (Jefferson, N.C.: McFarland, 1989) 32.

51. See the Appendix, pages 155–156.

52. D.J. Foskett, *The Creed of a Librarian: No Politics, No Religion, No Morals* (London: Library Association, 1962; reprint, London: Library Association, 1970) reprint 11.

53. Hauptman, *Professionalism or Culpability* 627.

54. Gilliam S. Gremmels, "Reference in the Public Interest: An Examination of Ethics," *RQ* 30 (Fall 1990) 365.

55. Michael Harris, "Portrait in Paradox: Commitment and Ambivalence in American Librarianship, 1876–1976," *Libri* 26 (1976) 281–301.

56. David Berninghausen, "Anthesis in Librarianship: Social Responsibility vs. The Library Bill of Rights," *Library Journal* 97 (November 15, 1972) 3675.

57. Betty-Carol Sellen, "Social Responsibility and the Library Bill of Rights: The Berninghausen Debate," *Library Journal* 98 (January 1, 1973) 27–28.

58.   Jane Robbins, "Social Responsibility and the Library Bill of Rights: The Berninghausen Debate," *Library Journal* 98 (January 1, 1973) 29.

59.   Clara S. Jones, "Social Responsibility and the Library Bill of Rights: The Berninghausen Debate," *Library Journal* 98 (January 1, 1973) 33.

Chapter 4

1.   Dee Garrison, "The Tender Technicians: The Feminization of Public Librarianship, 1876–1905," *Journal of Social History* 6 (1973) 131–159.

2.   Paul Bixler, "The Librarian—Bureaucrat or Democrat," *Library Journal* 79 (December 1, 1954) 2274–2279.

3.   American Library Association Office for Intellectual Freedom. *Intellectual Freedom Manual,* 4th ed. (Chicago: American Library Association, 1992) 16–24.

4.   *Rethinking Reference in Academic Libraries: The Proceedings and Process of Library Institute #2: University of California, Berkeley, March 12-14, 1993, Duke University, June 4-6, 1993,* facilitated by Louella Wetherbee, ed. by Anne Greodzins Lippo (Berkeley, Calif.: Library Solutions Press, 1993).

5.   Joan Durrance, "The Generic Librarian: Anonymity vs. Accountability," *RQ* (Spring 1983) 278–283.

Index